AN ADVENTURE SHARED

GW00728126

AN ADVENTURE SHARED

by

Catherine Baird

Salvation Books
The Salvation Army International Headquarters
London, United Kingdom

First published 1955 as *The Soldier*

Revised edition 2008

Copyright © 2008
The General of The Salvation Army

ISBN 978-0-85412-780-1

Cover design by Nathan Sigauke

Published by Salvation Books
The Salvation Army International Headquarters
101 Queen Victoria Street, London EC4V 4EH
United Kingdom

Printed by UK Territory Print & Design Unit

CONTENTS

SERIES INTRODUCTION
'CLASSIC SALVATIONIST TEXTS'

This series is intended to help a new generation of readers become familiar with works published across the years by The Salvation Army and which over time have come to be regarded as 'classics' in Salvationist circles and even beyond.

It is hoped also that these republications might lead to a rediscovery of them and the truths they convey by those who once read them. They live on not only for their content, but also for the passionate spirit that breathes through what is written.

Salvationists have no desire to live in the past, but we are ready to recognise the debt we owe to those who have gone before. We look to the future, under God, taking with us the sacred heritage he has given. These writings are part of that heritage.

I hope and pray that this series will help and inspire all who use it, and that some will be prompted to contribute in written form to modern Salvationist literature in an age that needs also the old, eternal truths expressed in language for the 21st century.

The series is dedicated to the glory of God.

Shaw Clifton
General
London, July 2007

FOREWORD

For many years, it has been my cherished dream to see Catherine Baird's wonderful book in print again so that children of the next generation could enjoy it. Everyone likes a story, and Catherine Baird was a born poet and storyteller. It helps of course, that she had intimate knowledge of this particular family!

Mary, the heroine, is heroic in the very best sense, displaying the quiet courage of a child of God – and the child of Salvation Army officers – in everyday events. We see life in Australia and South Africa from a child's viewpoint, which is humorous, adventurous and always perceptive. We follow the characters from babyhood through growth into young adults. We travel to the East End of London, England, observing The Salvation Army through the eyes of Walter, Mary's future husband. His journey takes him from a coffee stall in Victoria Dock Road to the training college for officers at Clapton and then out to South Africa on overseas service – where his path will cross with Mary's.

For more of the story, you will have to read the book! Everyone who has borrowed my copy has loved it, our own children included. May you enjoy it too!

Helen Clifton
Commissioner
World President of Women's Ministries
International Headquarters, London
March 2008

An Adventure Shared was originally published as *The Soldier* in 1955. 'Mary' the heroine, is Catherine Baird's elder sister, Winnie. 'Stephen' is her beloved brother, Sam. 'Mildred' and 'Sheila' are her sisters Jessica and Elsie. 'Elizabeth' ('Mother says she never had such a crying child') is Catherine herself. Older readers who want to know more about Catherine's life and writings should read *Pen of Flame* by John C. Izzard and Henry Gariepy, published by Crest Books, USA, in 2002.

One

Mary's Mother

Steadily forward march! To Jesus we will bring
Sinners of every kind, and he will take them in.

EVEN the loud, rhythmic beat of the drum and the jingle of tambourines could not drown the words of the song the marching Army sang as they tramped joyfully along the streets of Port Adelaide.

Beside the colour sergeant, Captain William Angus marched briskly. Underneath thick eyebrows, his blue eyes stared straight ahead, and when a rotten egg, like a playful golf ball, hit his chest and broke in a yellow mess over his crimson jersey his eyes never wavered, nor did he cease from singing. Taking a large, clean handkerchief from his coat pocket he vigorously wiped the jersey and sang in a rather untuneful voice, more loudly than ever: 'Sinners of every kind, and he will take them in.'

A shower of stones fell among the soldiers, fortunately hitting no one. The colour-sergeant deftly dipped the flag, and its crimson folds spread outward as he made a quick left turn and the Salvationists, following him, marched into single file till they stood in a large circle outside the hall.

'Brother White will pray,' said Captain Angus.

A former boxer with a face battered and scarred in the ring stepped forward, removed his Army cap and prayed, while flying eggs and stones mingled till it seemed as if a rain and hail storm had struck the praying group. Brother White spoke to God like a child speaking to his father. When he begged his Heavenly Father to 'save from sin the men who are stoning us now', his big, ugly face was gentle and earnest.

Before he turned to enter the hall door Captain Angus said 'Amen!' in a firm voice. As he walked up the aisle, a lighted piece of wood hurtled past him and fell on a child's head. Captain Angus ordered one of the sisters to look after the girl, and his steely eyes sought out the culprit, one of a row of larrikins seated on a form at the rear of the hall in readiness to begin a disturbance. On the floor beside him was a heap of thick, slimy substance used for causing the Salvationists to slip as they marched to their seats.

Without a word Captain Angus took the cloth cap from the larrikin's head, with it wiped the slime from the floor and, in swift unexpectedness, clapped it firmly on its owner's head. The peak covered the man's astonished eyes, so, before he knew what was happening, he felt himself being hoisted into the air, firmly gripped by his shirt collar and the seat of his trousers. He had time to marvel at the unsuspected strength of Angus who was slight and of average height, but who had the muscles of the builder he had been before he had joined the Army and began to build some of the first Salvation Army barracks in Australia.

When larrikin Dick Waller was firmly seated outside the hall Captain Angus went to the platform and opened the meeting. There was no disturbance that night, and many men and women came to the penitent form. But Dick Waller was not beaten. Followed by his gang he set off toward the quarters, a small weatherboard bungalow, where he knew Mrs Captain Angus and her new baby were alone. She, thought he, could not do battle with him and his followers.

From her bedroom Winifred Angus watched the noisy crowd, holding on to the rope, and charging toward the front veranda like wild buffaloes. They saw her face at the window and commenced to flourish the rope before her, grinning and making hideous faces. Four of the men were soon stationed at the front door and four at the back.

'The house'll be around your ears in a few minutes!' yelled Dick, banging on the window pane. Winifred quickly pulled down the venetian blind and slowly dressed in her blue uniform, carefully fastening the big silver shield at her throat. Then she lifted baby Mary from her cot and unhurriedly began to dress her. She could hear the roughs fastening the rope securely round the little house. She knew what they were going to do, for other

3

crowds of rowdies who did not like the new Army that had come to 'open fire' in Australia had, with a rope, pulled down the rather flimsy board houses in which some Salvationists lived.

Captain Angus always said that his wife measured four feet 11 inches, but she claimed an extra inch. Before she met the Army she had been a school teacher, easily managing the largest class of miners' children, and receiving recommendation for her ability to keep perfect order. Before her conversion her clear, soprano voice had charmed large audiences. Now, as she tied a silken bow on the baby's bonnet, she sang softly:

> *They bid me choose an easier path,*
> *And seek a lighter cross.*

Her voice soared up, becoming louder, till the men posted at the door must have heard the joyful ending of her song:

> *I cannot leave the dear old flag,*
> *'Twere better far to die.*

Like her husband she had steady, brave eyes, but hers were grey instead of blue, and they twinkled with fun and kindness more often than they burned with fighting fire.

The shouts outside became louder and more hilarious. A stone crashed through the window pane and fell against the blind. The baby, now being wrapped in a white shawl, tried to fix her roving eyes on her mother's face, and curled a row of tiny fingers around Winifred's thumb.

Mrs Angus ran her own fingers through her wavy, auburn hair and reached for her bonnet. She felt the walls of the house creak and a long, strained bellow, 'Pull boys!' from without.

Clasping Mary against her blue bodice, Winifred walked into the passage and opened the front door wide. Four burly forms standing there ready to plunge at her suddenly went limp as she crossed the threshold looking straight ahead, holding the baby as though she were just going for a walk.

Stepping over the taut rope, she nodded coolly at her tormentors. 'Good afternoon!' she said. 'You seem to be having some trouble, but I can't stop. I'm taking my baby to meet her father at the hall.'

'You dunderheads!' yelled Dick Waller, leaving the rope-pullers without a cheerleader while he dealt with his sentinels. 'What d'ya mean letting her get out? Tell me that!'

'Tell yourself!' they muttered, glowering at him.

Dick Waller's hands fell to his sides. He had been defeated by a slip of a girl – none other than Mary's mother.

Two

The Bet is Off

DICK WALLER'S jaw dropped, and he dared not look at his companions still standing on either side of the cottage doorsteps wondering what to do next. Though they wanted to, they could scarcely run from a woman and a baby, especially as a group of boys was already hooting them, and showering gravel among them.

Lifting his eyes, Dick saw a face with delicately chiselled features, and wavy auburn hair above grey twinkling eyes.

Like a military general passing through a guard of honour Mrs Angus walked, carrying Mary. The men stared after her until she turned the corner. Then they slunk away, but not in the direction of the hall, though some of them went there as soon as they dared, for a religion that gave a soldier's courage to a frail woman could not be mocked. The larrikins were indeed defeated.

When his wife came into the hall Captain William Angus was reading from the Bible. If he was surprised to see her there with the baby, he did not say so. He addressed a crowd of men and women who stared spell-bound at his message.

'I can do all things . . . ' he shouted as if he were Paul speaking boastfully. Then supposedly addressing the apostle he said firmly, 'Bet you half a crown, Paul, that's not true!' He searched his pocket for a half-crown, but found only a penny, and slammed it on the reading desk. For a while he leaned forward, staring at the pages of his Bible, but his voice was reverent, full of the wonder of what he was saying. 'Listen! "I can do all things through Christ which strengtheneth me"!'

Winifred, not wanting to disturb the gathering, sat at the back of the huge hall, but she could see the blueness of his eyes like fierce flames that never flickered. His voice became gentle. 'I apologise, Paul. I take back the half-crown. The bet is off. "I can do all things through Christ ... " That's different.'

Then he told the drunkards, the gamblers, the dishonest, the self-righteous and selfish that he knew how they despaired of overcoming in their own strength, but that with Christ they could do the impossible.

As he closed his Bible, he called Winifred to come to the platform and sing. Without a word she went up to him, placing Mary in his arms against the red jersey. Then, looking and sounding like one of the choirboys in the great church in which she had formerly worshipped, she sang:

Christ is all, yes, all in all,
My Christ is all in all.

Men hurried forward. A woman with scented garments and jewelled rings on her fingers knelt at the penitent form, took off her picture hat and cut out the ostrich feather that adorned it. From the back of the hall, men leaped over the seats in their haste to find God and discover how Jesus Christ his Son could help them to conquer sin.

Long before she was old enough to speak Mary loved the sound of tambourines and drums. She was a small, dainty child, with large blue eyes, burning like her father's, and fine, straight hair that was always held back with a ribbon from her high, wide forehead.

No one had to tiptoe about the house for fear of awakening her, for noise never troubled Mary. Behind the platform at the hall, she lay on a clean, soft bed made by her mother who must now always be with father in the meetings. There, all alone, she heard the jingle of tambourines and the shouting of the soldiers giving their testimonies. Every Sunday more soldiers spoke, for the corps was growing apace, and the roughs were in the minority. Besides, so many once notoriously wicked people were now good that the citizens of Port Adelaide would not allow anyone to interfere with the Salvationists.

As soon as she was old enough Mary sat on the Army platform beside her mother, and watched men and women who were tired of being drunkards, of stealing and lying, hurry to the Army penitent form to ask God to forgive them for all the wrong of the past.

The captain had a beautiful rosewood box that grandfather, Mother's father, had made, and Mary liked him to show her the treasures it held. There was a photograph of the colour-sergeant, who had been a boxer before his conversion. He had thick arms folded over a bare muscular chest. Mary thought how much nicer he looked in his blue uniform and crimson jersey, carrying the Army flag. In the box was a rosary which a man had left at the penitent form one night when he found he could speak to God without using it.

There were counterfeit coins, dice and many other articles men and women had once used dishonestly. Captain Angus kept them, for he and Winifred did not stay in Port Adelaide, and when they were working in other towns anything that reminded him of the men and women who in his meetings had been remade by God was valuable. When he talked of them his eyes burned more brilliantly.

Before Mary was five a baby sister and a brother had joined the family, Mildred and Stephen. With tea to prepare and a trio of lively children to put to bed, Winifred Angus sometimes could not go with her husband to the evening meeting, and Mary loved to lie awake till he came home. Then she would listen to him talking over the meetings with Mother. If men and women had come to the penitent form they were always very happy, and Mother would sing in a clear, high voice as she prepared the supper. Generally the meal was simply bread and butter, for Captain and Mrs Angus, like all early-day Salvation Army officers, were poor.

One night Mary heard Mrs Angus saying that the children needed new clothes. 'Mildred's toes are coming through her shoes,' she said sadly, 'and they all need new nightdresses.'

'I have only sixpence to give you,' said William Angus. 'But God will surely help us.'

'I can never take anything from the people,' said Winifred. 'Never, William, never.' The determination in her clear voice, without a doubt, matched the Army Mother's, though the circumstance in which she spoke was different.

'Perhaps God has no other way of providing for us, except through converted people,' Mary heard her father say. But no answer came from her mother.

A loud knock at the front door made Mary run to open it. Already she knew how to turn the big key in the lock, how to swing open the door and say politely, 'Good morning, ma'am, I will call my mother.'

A tall lady was standing outside. Mary knew her as the lady who owned the drapery shop. She looked right over Mary's smooth head at Winifred hurrying along the passage.

'Mrs Angus,' said the lady, 'God has been so good to me since you came here and, in gratitude, I've brought these rolls of flannelette and nainsook.

They might be useful for the children. Will you accept them?'

Mary heard the pleading note in the lady's voice and she looked anxiously at her proud mother who once had been able to give lavishly to others. There was a long silence; Mary could not know that her mother was fighting a battle with pride. But when Winifred took the roll of flannelette Mary felt happy, because the lady's face seemed to shine like a porcelain vase with a candle burning in it.

'Thank you,' she heard her mother say. 'I believe you have come from God, and I cannot refuse what he sends.'

For many nights when Mary was awake she heard the hum of Mrs Angus's sewing machine, and often she would awaken in the morning to discover her mother sewing long tucks into white pinafores, feather-stitching narrow hems and singing:

Christ is all, yes, all in all,
My Christ is all in all.

Three

Christ is All

MARY'S mother had not always sung 'Christ is all'. She had not always worn an Army bonnet. In fact, because her brother had donned the uniform of a Salvation Army captain she had once haughtily passed him in the street, without even a smile.

Winifred Anstey had sung at many concerts; sometimes she had sung 'The Holy City' or 'Vital Spark of Heavenly Flame'. At other times she had trilled happy songs, popular in her girlhood. In her mind, singing and religion had small relationship, but she had a soprano voice of rare quality and sing she must.

Like her father and mother, Winifred had been confirmed in the Anglican communion. She loved the liturgy. Her sense of beauty was satisfied in the silent, lofty church with its long nave, panelled walls and tall candles burning on either side of the altar. Sunday after Sunday her wine-coloured silk dress had faintly rustled as she walked down the aisle to the family pew, and many friendly eyes watched her serious face when she listened to the sermon, or watched, with an elder sister's critical, but kindly eye, her brothers John, Bert and George singing in the choir.

Winifred loved the dignity and grace of the church service. She revered the vicar's goodness as well as his scholarliness.

That she or her family would ever do more than laugh at the Salvationists singing in the streets never occurred to her. Everybody knew Winifred's father, John Anstey, and the three sons who assisted in his workshop. Winifred had always been proud of his medieval carving, some of which could be seen in London's St Paul's Cathedral and in other great English cathedrals in Salisbury, Wells and Durham. Their home had been and still was, beautified by his work, and everyone loved the tall, thin Manxman who, in the privacy of home, repeated the Lord's Prayer in his native tongue, and taught Winifred to do the same.

With her parents she had travelled from Liverpool to Sydney and then to Adelaide on a sailing vessel that tossed the seas for three months making the crossing. Mr Anstey had been proud of Winifred's ability to read the Bible at the age of four. He had taught her while she sat among the shavings on the floor of his workshop. In days when the education of girls was often neglected, John Anstey had decided that Winifred should have the best tuition available. When she had chosen to be a schoolteacher his joy had been complete, though he was sorry that in one of her first posts she had to live away from home.

Only vaguely had Winifred been aware of the Army. She heard their drums and singing in the distance and, if she thought of them at all, she regarded them as vulgar, even blasphemous.

One day she had received a letter in which her mother told her that John Anstey and she had 'joined the Army'. That was a shock which she had borne quietly; but when she had gone home for the summer holidays, she had found the whole family attending Army meetings every night. And, incredible though it seemed, when Bert had left the choir and the church, explaining that he had been converted in the Army and felt his place was there, the Bishop of Adelaide had laid his hand on the boy's head and blessed him.

Her bedroom had been loaned to two girl converts with a black past. Their clothes had lain in her treasured cedar chest. 'The family has gone mad!' Winifred had told herself, pondering over the difference between the rough, noisy crowd at the Army hall and the decorous occupants of the church pews, and fuming inwardly at the thought of disreputable strangers in her room. Curious, she had stood near an open-air meeting one night. She had seen John Anstey, tall, with refined bearing, wearing a red jersey and lustily singing with the others:

> *His blood can make the foulest clean,*
> *His blood avails for me.*

Then a burly individual had approached him and, slapping him on the shoulder, had said loudly, 'Come on, old gimlets, let's have your testimony.'

'Gimlets!' Winifred's short upper lip had curled in disgust. Gimlets indeed! Her father. She had pictured him bending over an eagle, carving till at last, from a block of wood, an eagle was fashioned, with a thousand feathers in each wing. 'Gimlets!' In her anger she had nearly choked as she had hurried home. Whatever would Friedrich von der Waaide think of this, she had raged, remembering suddenly how deep was her friendship with the young German schoolteacher who, with his violin, often accompanied her singing. Thinking of him she had begun to sing softly in German as he had taught her, *'Wenn die Schwalben heimwarts flieg'n'.*

She had hastened back to school resolved never again to come home. Then Kate Anstey, never very strong, had become so seriously ill that, at her mother's request, Winifred had unwillingly relented and returned to Adelaide. When she arrived home Kate was dead. Kate's illness had begun with a severe chill contracted one stormy night when she had gone out to see an old friend in an effort to win him for God. Winifred, kneeling beside her dead sister, regarding her capable hands so lately occupied in serving others, had promised God that if he would forgive all her sins and pride, she would take Kate's place as a soldier in The Salvation Army.

At the penitent form she had taken off her black picture hat and the ostrich feather that adorned it, and when she had returned to school she had worn a red Army blouse and a large silver shield. Friends who had sought her companionship and had counted it a privilege to be with her, had forsaken her. Friedrich, too, had slipped out of her life. At recess she had wandered alone in the playground. Soon, however, one friend, a Roman Catholic teacher, had come to her. 'Shall you be attending your open-air meeting tonight?' she inquired kindly.

'Yes,' Winifred had answered steadily.

'Then, I'm coming with you. I won't be able to stand in the ring, but I'll be just behind you, supporting you in your stand for what you believe to be right.'

Winifred had never forgotten her Roman Catholic friend, and when once again she lived in Adelaide she had often remembered her loyalty, while cabbage stumps and refuse of all kinds had dropped around the Salvationists testifying to how God had changed them.

Winifred had been shy in speaking of her own experience, and had admired those who were bold, especially a young Scot with a red beard and burning blue eyes. He was William Angus, hailing from Glasgow so recently that he often wore kilts of Robertson tartan. God had spoken to him through what the Salvationists, preaching and praying on a street corner in Adelaide, said about the holiness of God and the awfulness of sin, his sin. When he had found her, he had thought Winifred was an angel; she had thought he was a saint; and when – after both had learned to be good soldiers – he asked her to be his wife, she had said 'Yes'.

Winifred and William had married and had been accepted together as officers in The Salvation Army. Of course William discovered that Winifred wasn't the kind of angel he had pictured her. He found that, to do what she thought right, she would oppose even him. An angel, he discovered, was not one who agreed with everything he said. But he had come to see that an angel always turned his thoughts toward goodness and purity, always cheerfully accepted hardship with him for the sake of right, rather than ease and success away from God, and at the price of a cherished ideal.

Winifred, on the other hand, discovered that a saint is not a flawless statue, but a living being capable of leaving the narrow way a Christian must tread, yet by the grace of God giving his life in an effort to remain in that way.

William and Winifred were very different from each other, but they had one aim: to do God's will; so, even when they were sad they were happy, for to each and to both Christ had become all.

'Fancy Winifred Anstey sacrificing her voice!' friends had murmured. But when she heard their words Winifred made no reply. They meant, by sacrifice, that she had thrown her gift away. She realised that, as William had offered his energy and skill in building, so she had offered her voice and her gift for teaching.

One of the first things she taught Mary was that the only worthwhile way of life is doing God's will.

Four

The Dedication

STEPHEN was going to be dedicated to God and the Army. Mary was happy. She wore a clean, white dress and white socks and, with a feeling of excitement, she watched her mother putting a fresh silk handkerchief inside the collar of her uniform. Something big was about to take place, and Stephen was the centre of it. Sitting on a chair beside the bed, Mary stroked Stephen's tiny square hands and patted the long white gown he wore.

Mrs Angus had told her this was the robe she had worn when they had dedicated her to God. Mary was not at all sure what dedication meant as a word but she knew Stephen was going to be given to God. This was, in a way, rather puzzling, because she knew that Mother had asked God for a son, and God had promised her one.

Mrs Angus was sure of God. She even remembered the moment when the promise came, and she had lifted her hand from the wheel of the sewing machine, raised her face, closed her merry eyes and had prayed, 'Thank you, God. I will name him Stephen and he shall be yours in a special way.' So many times Mary had heard her mother describe her conversation with God that a picture of the scene was engraved on her mind and she never looked at Stephen without seeing it. Stephen had no second name as his sisters had, for Mother had not mentioned any other names to God when he had made his promise and she had made hers. He was just Stephen Angus.

Mary knew a little about the Stephen in the New Testament. He had loved Jesus, and because of his love he had been stoned by men who hated Jesus. She was anxious as she looked at her sleeping brother for she had heard her mother say that while she and Father were going to give Stephen to God, some day, after Stephen had learned to love Jesus, he would give himself. Would Stephen be stoned ever? Mary's oval face became serious as she wondered. But it was time to go to the hall and in the joy of watching beside the pram she forgot to be troubled.

Major John Dean had travelled from Sydney to Bulli to dedicate Stephen. Forty miles was nothing to John Dean, Father said. He travelled all over the country, over parched land or muddy paddocks, visiting people in huts and telling everyone he met about God.

Mary watched him striding up and down the platform, very tall and thin with big, dark, shining eyes. She did not know what he was saying to the people but she knew it must be important, for some of them looked frightened. When she saw him call her mother and father to stand before him with

Stephen she hoped her little brother would be safe, that the long arms, lately waving about as he preached, would not crush the baby. She hoped the dark-faced preacher would not hurt her mother. No one could frighten her – that was certain.

From a little red book Major Dean read: 'If you wish the Lord so to take possession of the soul and body of this child, that he shall only and always do his will, you must be willing that he should spend all his life in salvation war wherever God may choose to send him; that he should be despised, hated, cursed, beaten, kicked, imprisoned or killed for Christ's sake.

'You must let him see in you an example of what a Salvation Army soldier ought to be, and teach and train him, to the best of your ability, to be a faithful soldier, giving all the time, strength, ability and money possible to help on the war.

'You must keep as far from the child as you can all intoxicating drink, tobacco, finery, wealth, hurtful reading, worldly acquaintance and every influence likely to injure him either in soul or body; and you must carry out to the best of your ability the will of God and the wishes of your superior officers with respect to him.'

Mary knew nothing about drink, tobacco, finery or wealth. She had seen none of these things; but she knew people were hated, stoned, imprisoned and killed for Christ's sake.

One of her father's friends had died as a result of a brick thrown at him in an open-air meeting. Only yesterday Lieutenant Luckerman and Lieutenant Richardson had been charged in the Wallongon court with violating a by-law by parading the streets. They had been sent to prison for two months. Would Stephen go to prison because he was God's?

In her imagination Mary heard her father reading from *The War Cry* an account of the trials of the Salvationists who wanted everybody to know about God who could make them happy and good. Captain Angus had been pleased that the man who wrote in *The War Cry* courageously expressed his opposition to the thoughtlessness of men who made money by selling beer to men and women too weak and stupid to refuse it.

Father had also been delighted with another lieutenant who had told the magistrate the Army drum was the property of the Lord. 'So it is,' said Father with blazing eyes that Mary's were beginning to match.

A shaft of sunlight made a golden broadening way from the top of the window to the place where Captain and Mrs Angus stood under the flag. Mary's mother was placing Stephen in the arms of the tall, dark major. Mary waited, breathless. Would he hurt Stephen?

The long arms almost covered the white-robed babe, and the voice once loud as a storm at its height, was gentle as a cool breeze, deep and full of love. In the sunlight Major Dean stood holding up

Stephen and saying: 'O Lord God, take this child Stephen Angus to be thine own!'

Mary felt very small in the silence. Would God say 'Yes' in a voice like thunder? But there was no sound. A wonderful event was taking place. They were in the presence of the God who made the world, the stars, the beautiful gum trees, the blue skies. What was he like? Mary could not imagine, but Mother had said Jesus was like him, and she knew that Jesus blessed children long ago in Palestine, and that made her sure God was touching Stephen now.

Stephen was God's, thought Mary. But, when he could talk and understand, he must give himself. Then she remembered that she had been dedicated to God, and already she could talk and understand. Why, she was even old enough to be left at home to watch beside the cradle and to be trusted with the big key of the front door. She could even turn it in the lock.

She would give herself to God. She wanted to even if she had to go to prison like Lieutenant Richardson or be stoned like Stephen. These things would be as nothing compared with the joy of belonging to God.

Five

Crab Holes

MARY drew the curtain aside, laying her cheek against clean, white lace. Mrs Angus always said that a dirty window and bedraggled curtain were signs to passers-by that unhappy people lived in the house, so Mary was usually interested in windows and window drapes. But this morning she scarcely gave the newly laundered lace a thought; she wanted to look at the yellow buggy standing outside the quarters and to watch Father harnessing Topsy, the new pony, to the long shafts.

Topsy and the buggy had been given to Captain and Mrs Angus by friends who were interested in what Australian Salvationists called a camp or central post, from which 15 or 20 other posts were operated. A Salvationist was in charge of each post but Captain Angus visited them often, and sometimes he was away from home for as long as two weeks.

This wintry day Mary, Mildred and Stephen were going to ride in the buggy with Father and Mother along dignified streets, past suburban villas, through hills and beside the river, and away into the Australian bush. Mary had helped her mother pack soap, tea, sugar, matches, billy-cans and brush and curry-comb and changes of clothing. She had even helped Father carry out the water-bags, blankets and jack-knives. When the tent had been folded she had patted the canvas sides and trotted back to the kitchen to see that nothing had been forgotten.

One by one the three children were lifted into the buggy. Mary sat in the centre with one arm around Mildred, the other around Stephen. Mother tied a dust veil over her Army hat and under her chin; Father took the reins, whistled to Topsy and they were off, with Mary listening to the eager clip, clip, clop, clop, clip, clip clop of Topsy's feet, and enjoying the wind on her cheeks and in her soft, fine hair. She called Stephen and Mildred to look at the twittering parakeets seeming to greet the family as they drove along.

When weariness made Mary loosen her hold of Stephen, Captain and Mrs Angus brought Topsy to a standstill. By the roadside the tent was pitched and a fire lighted from sticks Mary had gathered, but before tea was brewed in the big billy-can, Mary's tired eyes had closed and she was asleep on the ground with her young sister and brother, covered with a canopy of mosquito netting.

She awoke longing to explore the bush but too hungry and thirsty to wander far from the tent. Mary thought nothing had ever tasted so refreshing as the Cornish pasties mother laid out for her on a clean tablecloth spread in front of the tent. But

Topsy was harnessed and the family was off again along a road stretching through ploughed land which, Mary thought, was like a sea of chocolate. She was still thinking of this when the buggy lurched to one side, then to the other. Her right arm tightened around Stephen; her left hand clasped Mildred's warm, fat palm. Topsy whinnied and flung up her head. Father's eyebrows and moustache seemed to bristle; but Mother's face was calm.

'A crab hole,' Mary heard her father say, and she knew they were in danger. There were many crab holes in the district, the result of volcanic eruption throwing up numerous tiny hillocks all over the country and leaving deep holes into which the rain poured. The huge cavity filled with mud and sometimes appeared to be firm ground, so that neither horse nor driver noticed it. In one of these holes Topsy now struggled, with nostrils widening and muscles quivering as she mustered all her strength in an effort to leap from the mire. But the harder the frantic beast worked the further into the mud she sank. Handing the reins to his wife, Captain Angus leaped to solid ground and grasped Topsy's bridle, but her wild eyes seemed not to see him, for she was now in a wild panic, feeling herself being sucked downward as in quicksand.

Stephen's eyes were round and surprised; Mildred was crying, but Mary looked at Mother whose face was still untroubled, and she was not afraid. Soon she was alone in the buggy with her charges, for

27

Mother, who had handled ponies since her childhood, was Topsy's special friend and Captain Angus believed she alone could calm the terrified animal.

As she sprung from the lurching buggy Father caught her in his arms and set her down beside him with her dust veil flowing back from her shoulders and her auburn curls lying against her white cheek. Like a girl she laughed, looking into Father's eyes, happy in an adventure shared with him. Then, as if moving swiftly from pleasure to work, she took Topsy's bridle in her strong, though small hand. 'Now Topsy,' she said. Topsy ceased lunging about and focused her eyes in the direction of the voice that gave her confidence. 'Jump, Topsy!' said Mrs Angus.

The harness creaked; with a terrific effort Topsy obeyed the order, and at last she dug her forefeet into solid ground, though her sides heaved with the exertion. Mrs Angus called and encouraged until trembling, but triumphant, Topsy drew the buggy safely to the firm road. The pony drooped her head and pressed her nose into Mother's hand. 'Good Topsy,' Mother said, 'Good girl.' Father lifted the children to the ground, giving Mary a gentle hug. 'Not every little girl would have been so patient,' he said.

When the pony had rested they travelled on, arriving at last at a canvas shed near a schoolhouse where the meeting was to be held. Wagon-loads of

Salvationists from other posts arrived, until a great procession formed and marched around the town which consisted of one house and the school. Mary forgot about the crab hole. She knew the journey home would be a happy one for she had heard how the sergeants in charge of the posts were being welcomed by the bush dwellers, of how they eagerly read *The War Cry* and *The Young Soldier* and received the gospel message, of isolated homes where Army caps hung beside the open fireplaces, that the crimson jerseys of Salvationists were seen more frequently in the bush than in the city, and of Salvationists tending fever-ridden men lying alone in tents far from medical aid.

Best of all that night, in the meeting led by Captain and Mrs Angus, seven men and women had knelt at the penitent form giving themselves to God. Mary remembered them long after she had forgotten the crab hole. She went to sleep happily on the first night home from the bush.

In the morning a letter lay on the breakfast table. Mother said it contained Farewell Orders. A big chest Father had made to hold his books was in the middle of the floor, for although Farewell Orders only told Captain and Mrs Angus they were going to move and they might have to wait several days until Marching Orders came telling them to where they were going, they had begun to pack. Officers in God's Army do not ask questions; they go when and where they are sent because, said Mary's mother, 'We are in God's will.' That meant, thought Mary, that they lived right in God's heart. She would like to be there, too. Again she remembered the dedication, and was thoughtful.

Six

Mother and Mary Have a Secret

IN the corner of an oblong box made of bird's-eye maple and inlaid with a black-patterned border, Mother and Mary had a secret. Mary enjoyed having a secret, especially this one, for it concerned everybody in the house. Mother said that soon another baby was coming to be theirs, and in the maplewood box was the money to pay for the dresses and bonnets, vests and shawls all babies needed – a layette, Mother called it.

Sometimes, when the rent of the hall and the house was paid, the oil bought for the big brass lamp that hung in the barracks or stood on the dining-room table at home, Father would bring home a pound, a shining golden sovereign, and slap it down on the kitchen table in front of Mother as though it were a fortune. Her eyes would twinkle then, and she and Mary would exchange glances and think of the maplewood box and the bag of silver coins that lay in it.

To change that glittering sovereign into less beautiful coins seemed a pity, thought Mary; but it had to be done. First, from the pound a tenth had to be subtracted – the Lord's money, Captain and Mrs

Angus called it. Some of the tenth went into white envelopes, called cartridges, some was put aside for the children to give in the collection at the junior meeting. Some was saved lest a needy man or woman should require help. Then there were groceries to buy, and shoes and wool for the socks that Mother knitted. After that Mother put a shilling aside for the layette.

She had saved almost enough to buy two-ply wool and fine nainsook when Marching Orders came to go to a distant town and Captain and Mrs Angus did not have enough money in the corps funds to pay their fare. They must pay it themselves, for no other way seemed right to them.

Mother was very quiet when she and Father made the decision. As she gathered their few personal belongings together, Father packed them as meticulously and proudly as he once, as a builder, had laid bricks and stones in their places. Mary heard Mother tell him not to worry about the fare, for she had saved a little.

Father's blue eyes opened wide. 'Saved? How, Winifred?'

'Oh, in the usual way – hoarding in a box – this box as a matter of fact.' She passed him the maplewood box and told him to look inside. With an expression like Stephen's when he peered into the biscuit barrel, Captain Angus put his hand over the bag of shillings and sixpences. Mary held her breath, for to her this was sacred money, and it was going to be used to buy railway tickets. Could that be right? she wondered. But she must not stand and gaze. The oldest in a family of Salvationists is always busy, even when she is only seven.

Quietly Mary went into the kitchen and began to pile up the tea plates and cups ready for washing. She took the kettle from the hob and fastened it to a suspended hook, letting it hang nearer the red coals. Soon the water boiled and Mother came to pour it into a large tin basin. Mrs Angus told her she need not worry about the money that must be used for travelling. God would provide for the baby.

After a silence she said, 'We shall all have to be careful in the new place, for a young man has been appointed as Father's lieutenant; he will be sharing our food and our salary.' Even Mother sounded a little worried about this, but Mary knew now that if God could provide for the baby he would also provide for the lieutenant.

Lieutenant Cook came to the station to meet Father and Mother. He was a tall young man with a friendly face, and though they all walked from the train to the quarters, he carried Stephen all the way, and Stephen, who would never let strangers touch him, played with the 'S's on his collar. By the time the family arrived at the quarters, the little boy and the big man were friends.

Lieutenant Cook, Mary heard her mother say, had given up a well-paid post to be an officer in God's Army. That was as much as she knew. He and

Mother often talked about books and music. He seemed to know a great deal but on Fridays he put on a white apron like the one the grocer wore, rolled up the sleeves of his jersey, piled up the furniture of each room in turn and scrubbed the quarters floors till the boards seemed to shout their cleanliness. Then he polished everything he could find to polish, and presented himself to Father, once again the uniformed lieutenant with a bundle of copies of *The War Cry* over his arm.

One day while he was out with the Army's papers the postman delivered a large parcel, addressed in a strange handwriting to 'Mrs Captain Angus'.

Mary carried it proudly into the dining-room to Mother, who untied the knots and removed the thick brown paper. Neatly packed in a square box were long white gowns, baby vests, a cream cashmere pelisse and bonnet trimmed with white fur – everything and much more than Mother's money would have bought.

Mary touched the pelisse as if it were sacred. 'Did God send it, Mother?' she asked. But Mrs Angus was standing with her hands clasped and her face lifted. Her face seemed to shine. Mary closed her eyes, too.

'Do you remember how we thought we might not have enough for Lieutenant as well as ourselves, Mary?' Mother asked.

Mary remembered.

'Well, all these lovely clothes have been sent to us by his sister.'

Mary understood. Father had said long ago that God provided their needs through converted people, and because Mother accepted what he said she had told Mary.

After a long, thoughtful silence, 'Mother, would God have sent the baby's clothes if you hadn't saved up, and if there had been no fare to pay?'

'I don't know,' Mary's mother replied. 'But I do know that God expects us all to do our part in looking after ourselves and those he gives us to look after.'

Mary nodded. This seemed fair. In the Angus household everyone helped the other. Mary could not take part in a meeting but she could hurry home and, with the big key, open the door, let herself in and put the kettle on the iron bars that stretched from hob to hob of the wide, coloured fireplace.

When Mother came she did all the work that was too difficult for Mary. Father, on the other hand, did those things that were too hard for Mother. Early on Monday mornings he took an axe and chopped tree logs into short lengths. Small Stephen carried them one by one until in the woodshed there was a pile large enough to last the week. Mary helped Stephen to manage coat buttons and shoe-laces, but he was learning quickly to do this for himself.

'Suppose,' said Mary, 'you had saved the money and not had to pay the fare, would God still have told Lieutenant's sister to send the clothes?'

'I don't know,' Mother patiently answered again. 'But if he had, then he might have spoken to me about someone even poorer than we are.'

'If everyone listened to what God told them to do there wouldn't be any poor people in the world, would there, Mother?' she said, and went back to stroke the new garments.

After that, Mary loved Lieutenant Charlie Cook more than ever, and when he was ordered to another town she was not at all surprised that Stephen wanted to go with him. But when Sheila, the new baby, came, Stephen was glad he had not gone away, even with Charlie Cook.

Seven

Sheila

WET blankets were hung at every open doorway in the hope of lessening the burning heat of the wind blowing from the direction of the bush. The house was almost silent except for an occasional bump or a muffled shout from the room where Mildred and Stephen were playing.

Sheila was ill and would take no food. Mary had never seen her mother so worn and white as she was now. She seemed not to rest at all, and though Mary, who generally stayed with the younger children while Mrs Angus went with the Captain to the meetings, was glad not to be without her, the sight of the baby lying in her cot, turning her head from side to side and whimpering feverishly, troubled her so that she tossed in her sleep, and once was found, fast asleep, lifting Sheila out of her bed.

Mother had sent for the doctor, who told her that Sheila had pneumonia. At night, after the meeting, Captain Angus watched beside the baby while Mother snatched a few hours' sleep. During the day Mary did her best to keep the rooms tidy and the young children so amused that they were no trouble to her mother. No one noticed her efforts, but that never troubled Mary, for she scarcely thought of herself. Every morning, before the sun was too hot, she put on a big cotton sun-bonnet and, with a basket over her arm, went early to the butcher and baker and, because she was still too small to carry heavy baskets of groceries, made several trips to the grocer.

As the days passed, Sheila became more feverish so Captain Angus called at the doctor's house and asked him to call at the quarters.

The doctor stared at Father's red jersey as if he did not like its flaming colour or the message of the yellow crest. 'I'm too busy,' he snapped. 'Bring her here.'

'I ask you to come,' said Captain Angus fixing on the unwilling doctor the fiery gaze that had made many larrikins quail. In his opinion a doctor who did not fulfil the promises of his noble profession was as deeply in need of a pardoning God as any ignorant larrikin. Turning on his heel, he walked briskly from the surgery. Half an hour later, the jingling bell attached to the doctor's gig announced his arrival. Stalking angrily into the house, he was met by Mrs Angus with Sheila in her arms. 'Put her down somewhere!' the doctor said. Mrs Angus laid the baby on a folded white shawl on the scrubbed kitchen table.

Glancing at her, the doctor said, 'Gum fever. She's teething, that's all.'

Mother's face whitened. 'Dr Saunders,' she said, 'you told me Sheila had pneumonia.'

'Then she has,' he said. 'Take this prescription to the chemist and if there's no change call me.' He held out the prescription to Mother but, as she was looking past him, he laid it on the table and went out. Captain Angus followed him to the door, closing it firmly after him. Then he went back to Mother who was kneeling beside the baby, praying, her head drooped on her arms. Captain Angus slipped quietly away. He always knew when Mother wanted to be alone.

Mary watched her mother rise from her feet and tear up the prescription. Then she laid Sheila on a pillow because her baby was too thin to be carried in the ordinary way. Wet with perspiration, her hair curled over the forehead, but she did not attempt to brush it back. No air seemed now to stir the wet blankets in the doorway and on the veranda. So Sheila was taken into the back yard, where Mother paced up and down unsmiling and weary but with a look of quietness on her face that Mary understood. She knew she must not talk.

For nearly an hour Mother walked up and down the dusty path, up and down till the sound of her feet became part of the sound of the everyday, something permanent. In the kitchen Mary, playing with Mildred and Stephen, was suddenly aware of silence. Her mother had stopped pacing up and down. Then, she heard a voice saying cheerily, 'Mrs Angus, can I do anything for you?'

Over the top of the fence a fair head showed – Mrs Blake's head. In her garden a small girl, fat and rosy, was playing with a ginger kitten.

'I've tried everything, but Sheila will take nothing,' Mother said. Then she told Mrs Blake about the doctor who did not seem to remember what he had said one day from the other.

Mary did not hear all that the two women said but she saw Mrs Blake run into her own kitchen while Mother sat on the edge of the well, looking down at Sheila, less weary-looking, less sad.

Soon, on the other side of the fence, the fair head appeared. Mother stood up and took from Mrs Blake a baby's shining bottle filled with creamy-coloured liquid. 'This food saved my baby's life,' Mary heard Mrs Blake say. 'Yours may like it too. We can but try.' Suddenly feeling happy and cool in spite of the heat, Mary ran into the yard.

Mother, sitting on the side of the well again, was gently pressing the rubber teat into Sheila's lips. They closed over it and she began to suck wearily at first, then faster and faster. As she curved her lips she looked up at her mother with a surprised look in her eyes. Fascinated, Mary saw the decreasing contents of the bottle, and at last it was all gone.

'There, that's done it,' cried the owner of the fair head and bobbed down on her side of the fence. 'Thank you, God!' Mary heard from Mother. The kitchen door banged shut and open, shut and open, the hot wind was stirring again, gathering strength which in five minutes would dry the wet blankets, and more would have to be hung out, but nothing mattered. Mary heard her father's key in the front door – she ran to meet him.

'Sheila is better! Sheila is better!' she shouted. He caught her in his arms, and when he set her down she skipped beside him along the passage and out to the well.

Eight

And the Rains Came

MARY liked to hear rain pattering on the roof when she was safely in bed. She often tried to stay awake to enjoy the sound of cheery talk between Father and Mother, and the comfortable feeling of the clean sheets and blankets, but generally she was so tired that she fell asleep quickly. Tonight, however, the rain did more than patter on the roof; it roared so that, although Mary fell asleep, she soon wakened from dreaming that hosts of larrikins were hammering on the roof and shaking the window.

Slipping out of bed she peered through the window, trying to see into the darkness. Rain, like huge sheets, sloped downwards and the yard was a dark, shining pool, with little fountains of water spraying upward wherever the downpour met its surface. Mary knew that on the flats along the Hunter River, the farmers raised lucerne, maize and vegetables. In times of flood or drought she always remembered them. To her, the river was like a person whose moods changed. Sometimes the river person was gently useful, a meek creature, holding ships safely on her bosom as they carried their precious cargoes to and from Newcastle, 20 miles away. Sometimes she stormed and raged, or was dull and sullen.

Now, curled up, hearing the rain, Mary became aware of a dull, slow roar. Scarcely breathing she lay waiting while the roaring sound increased in volume, till it was like never ceasing thunder and other sounds were smothered. She did not hear the bedroom door open as Mrs Angus came in.

'Are you awake, Mary?' her mother asked with her lips close to the child's ear.

Mary searched the face near to her own, but she saw there no sign of anxiety or fear. In a voice that matched her mother's she replied, 'Yes, only wondering what the river is doing.'

'The river has burst its bank,' Mother said. 'I think we may all be needed soon, so you had better dress quickly and come into our room.'

Mary dressed while the roaring continued. The river, she thought, had changed into a thousand lions all rushing at the town. Any moment one of the lions might reach the front door – it had. She heard a thump, thump, thump, then a shout.

Standing behind her father while he opened the door, she could see Brother Brown, the corps secretary, clad only in pyjamas and overcoat, his face white, his hair lying wet over his forehead. He stumbled into the room moaning, 'My books, my books; they're all gone. The river's taken in a few minutes what I've gathered in a lifetime.'

He broke down, sobbing. Without being told to do so Mary went into the kitchen to make him a cup of tea. As she waited for the water to boil, she reflected that, though he was scarcely dressed and had lost his home and everything in it, he wept only for the books. Books must be great treasures, she thought. No wonder Father packed his and Mother's so carefully whenever they moved.

As the hours passed, other faithful local officers came to the quarters, which was on high ground beyond the dreadful area where tables, chairs and even the bodies of animals and some people floated on the rising tide as it lapped over verandas and burst through doors and windows. One soldier had rushed his wife and children from a house flooded to the ceiling. Another who possessed one of the finest farms in the district left it completely submerged. Later, when the water receded, all the results of his labours were swept away or smothered in 12 inches of sand, and he with neighbours facing similar losses stood sobbing as they gazed on the destruction.

Mary never forgot the sorrowful little company and the sensible, quiet way they acted during the night, helping her mother prepare shakedowns for the grown-ups and beds for the children.

During the next few days the hall was a home for about 150 people. As Mary watched her father and mother folding the blankets sent by the town council, and arranging long trestle tables in preparation for a hot meal now being cooked over the oven fire, she felt glad to be allowed to do the smallest task, to be a grain of sand helping to stem a tide of distress. She was thinking this when the hall door opened and a man came in. She liked him, for he had a face not unlike her father's, with thick, bushy eyebrows, very steady eyes and strong, broad shoulders.

He went about with Captain Angus among the people, talking over their losses, wondering over the way they were washing and ironing and even cooking in the Army hall, still cheerful. Alone with Captain and Mrs Angus, his grey eyes filled with tears. The Divisional Officer, Major Isaac Unsworth, had travelled through the stricken area seeing hundreds of gaunt-faced, hungry people and frightened children, having no one to explain the tragedy that had befallen them, walking barefoot through the streets - hundreds of country folk who had been brought by boat to the town and housed in public buildings. Major Unsworth had preached in the street to crowds who forgot their sorrows when they heard the good news of salvation. At Hexham a mother had taken her children to a high hill, but the rising waters had swept one little girl away and she had been drowned.

'Was that God's will?' whispered Mary.

'No,' said Mother, 'the flood, not God, took her body; but God received her spirit. She is in his care.'

'Could God stop the river?' Mary questioned.

'He will show men how they may prevent the river from overflowing, some day.'

Years later, when strong embankments were built along the river, Mary remembered her mother's words.

After that Mary did not worry about the many who had lost their lives in the flood. They were with God, who is love. God was also with the sad, poor people left behind and needing all that could be done for them. As she sat with Father at the big table and heard some of the refugees calling him 'Father' she thought God was working through him, and her heart nearly burst with pride. The whole town was his family and Mother's.

After dinner Major Unsworth opened the Bible and read the story of the man who built his house upon the sand, and when the rains came the house collapsed. Then he talked about the man who had built on a rock and whose house was still standing when the storm passed over.

Mary wondered if the people whose homes were lost in the flood would be hurt, thinking he meant that if they had been better people they might not have lost their homes, but they were not hurt. They knew Major Unsworth had chosen the occasion of sad tragedy to help them to understand that when our trust is in God, and not in our possessions, trouble and loss cannot hurt us.

At prayers that evening, Brother Brown who had lost everything began to pray. 'O God,' he said, lifting his face upward so that the light shone on his radiant features, 'Thou art our joy and our home.'

Mary knew what he meant.

Nine

A Baby or a Purse

MARY walked slowly down the veranda steps into the yard. Under one arm she carried a basket of baby's clothes which Mother had just washed in the big tub in the kitchen. Usually when she was hanging out the clothes she sang, but today was different. The new baby with the tiny head, now lying in a cradle Grandfather had made, was not her baby. She had been handed over to Mildred, who was eight.

Mary, now 10, knew all about babies. She had sat on the floor and rocked Mildred's wooden cradle; she had held the bottle while Stephen drank; when she was six, and mother was ill, she had walked up and down with flaxen-haired Sheila in her thin arms. Now Elizabeth was lying in the bedroom, asleep for once. She had a tiny, oval face and when she opened her eyes she seemed not to like the world at all. Her head was covered with silky, black hair which made her skin seem even whiter than it was.

Mary, who had been the first in the family to see her after the doctor left, wanted her more than she had ever wanted anything in her life. She wanted to tell Elizabeth that the world was, after all, a beautiful place; that there was a grey kitten in a cosy basket at the back of the woodshed where the wash-tubs hung; that a frog sometimes croaked beside the veranda steps and that it had once leapt on to her shoulder in a friendly way. She wanted to teach Elizabeth to read, to sew with neatness the hems of handkerchiefs and to play 'Santa Lucia', which she was practising now on the walnut piano, of which they were all proud because all had gone without something so that it could be paid for.

But it was no use. Mother had firmly said, 'No, Mary, you have Stephen and Sheila. The baby shall belong to Mildred, and Mildred must care for her when I am busy.'

Mildred was very pleased. She gave her thick, dark, curling hair a flick and walked around with little short steps, thinking how grand it would be to wheel the new baby to the park. She could almost hear the neighbours saying, 'What a lovely baby! Is she your sister?' And Mildred would say, oh very politely, 'Yes, Ma'am. She belongs to me – she's mine. I look after her.' What had happened the first time Mildred took Elizabeth out had given her a surprise.

Before she had reached the corner of the street, Elizabeth's dark head had moved on the white pillow. Then a pink fist had wriggled over the coverlet and a grunt announced dissatisfaction, Elizabeth's usual dissatisfaction with life. Mildred had joggled the pram wildly. Elizabeth had opened her eyes, looked at Mildred and had let out a yell; then she had begun to kick and twist until she and the pink coverlet had been like a screeching whirlwind of pink and white.

Mildred's dreams of ladies saying, 'What a lovely baby!' had flown. A neighbour with a thin face had come across the street, pushed Mildred aside, lifted out Elizabeth, smoothed the pillows, laid her down and had put back the pink coverlet.

'Don't you know how to look after your little sister?' she had said crossly, and had gone off, frowning.

When Mildred had brought back her charge, she had told Mary the sad tale, tears of anger rolling down her cheeks. Remembering, Mary tried not to laugh.

Setting down the clothes basket, she sighed, thinking of the dark head resting against the white pillow in the cradle. She tried not to be angry with Mildred for, after all, that would be silly. Mother was right. It was Mildred's turn to lift the baby out of the cradle; Mildred should have the joy of bringing out the white enamel bath, the pink soap-dish, the white towel with the blue rabbits on it – yes, this was right, Mary told herself. She pegged the clothes on to the line and they swung back and forth, white and sweet-smelling. Really, to be quite fair, she ought to have let Mildred hang out these clothes, but Mildred was much better at decorating the table for birthday teas than she was at pegging clothes on the line. Mary stooped to pick up some fallen pegs and when she looked at the clothes again they showed dry patches, for the day was sunny and the wind hot.

If she waited a while longer the clothes would all be dry and she could take them in. But no, she did not think she wanted to go into the house, for she could hear a small wailing cry, and it made her sad. That the baby was crying was not sad, for she knew babies often cried and that crying was good for them so long as it didn't mean they were in pain. Mary knew the difference between a cry that meant pain, an angry cry and a hungry cry. At this moment she knew that Mildred would be holding the baby. The angry cry now sounding meant that the new baby did not think much of Mildred as a nurse.

If she ran into the kitchen, Mrs Angus would say, 'No, Mary, the baby is in Mildred's care; she must mind her. You should be at your homework now.' Yet the wail became louder, and she could stand it no longer. She picked up the clothes pegs and ran faster, faster, up the steps and into the kitchen. The baby was lying on two pillows on the floor and Mildred was sitting beside her with one hand dangling a red rattle in front of her eyes, and in the other holding a book, trying to read.

'You ought to talk to her,' said Mary fiercely. 'She knows you aren't really thinking of her.'

Mildred put down the book. Her thick hair, of which she was rather proud, was unusually disordered and her face was flushed. 'She can howl for ever, for all I care,' she said.

'Mildred!' cried horrified Mary. Her big eyes opened so wide that they were like the pansies in the garden plot. 'If she's your baby, you've got to make her know you love her. Then she won't cry so much.'

Mildred picked up a half-eaten apple that she had put on the stool and began to munch. Between munches she said, 'Mother says she never had such a crying child.'

'That's because I'm not looking after her,' thought Mary, but she never said it, for Mildred's next remark shocked her even more than the first had done.

'And I don't see how I can make her know I love her when I don't.'

For a while Mary could not speak. Then, almost choking in an effort to keep back an angry rebuke, she said, 'Would you like me to mind her for you, just for a while.'

'I'd be jolly glad,' said Mildred, munching firmly.

So Mary sat down on the floor, taking the red rattle from Mildred and smiling down at Elizabeth, who looked at her out of eyes that said she didn't think much of the world, or even of Mary for that matter. Mary flattened herself down beside the baby and made cooing sounds. The wailing ceased. 'You do look stupid,' called Mildred, but Mary never heard.

At bedtime, Mary shook out the cradle coverlet and patted the white pillow. She brought the enamel bath and the pink soap-dish. She took the white towel with the blue rabbits on it from the baby's special towel rail. Then she ran to tell Mother that everything was ready for the bath.

'And where is Mildred?' asked Mother rather sharply.

Mary smiled. 'I borrowed the baby for this afternoon,' she said.

Mother wasn't altogether sorry; she often found Mildred's help more than a hindrance. Mary knew without being reminded how to test the baby's bathwater with the tip of her elbow, how to hold the baby so that she did not slip; she knew just when it was time to hand Mother the clean nightdress when the baby lay wriggling on her lap, complaining about the world and the things a baby had to endure.

After all, thought Mary as the days passed and she was still looking after Elizabeth, it doesn't matter if she belongs to Mildred, so long as I can look after her. Elizabeth was beginning to notice her now, and the grey eyes said that though their owner didn't think much of anything or anybody else, Mary, at least, was a very nice person.

One day a visitor gave Mary a silk purse. She liked it. On Saturdays when Mother gave her threepence for helping her all through the week, she opened the purse, slipped in the coin and felt quite grown up. Besides, the purse was beautiful. Mildred, too, thought it was beautiful. On the way home from school she begged Mary to give it to her; but Mary could not part with it. Not only did she like the purse, but she liked the friend who had made it for her.

Just before Christmas, when they went to bed at night, Mary and Mildred always had long talks about their plans. Father's and Mother's presents had to be made – handkerchiefs for Father and a needlecase for Mother, who had so many socks and stockings to darn. Money boxes had to be opened and pennies spent on books or trains for Stephen and dolls for Sheila. Then, somehow, Mildred and Mary had to find out what each other wanted. Often the pennies would not go far enough and the two eldest children had to give each other an old toy.

Remembering this, Mildred whispered, 'If you cannot buy a present for me, Mary, and you have to give me something you already have, could it be the silk purse?'

That evening the moon was shining brightly, and if there is a man in the moon he must have laughed to see the expression on Mary's face. She had a happy thought. 'Mildred,' she said, hugging herself tightly. 'But, Mildred, you have Elizabeth.'

'But I don't want Elizabeth,' said Mildred. 'I haven't wanted her for a long while. She's always crying, and I hate helping to bath her and rock her to sleep. I'd rather have the purse a thousand times.'

'Then,' said Mary, 'will you give Elizabeth to me?'

'Ooh yes!' cried Mildred. 'You can have her now, before Christmas.'

Mary received Elizabeth, the baby who cried a great deal and who looked at the world as if she did not like it, but who soon loved Mary so much that no one else was allowed to dress her, to take her out or to put her to bed – Elizabeth who might learn to sew, to play with the kitten, to darn, to read, to play 'Santa Lucia'.

On Christmas morning Mrs Angus saw the purse at the top of Mildred's stocking. 'That will be treasured by Mildred, for you valued it a lot, Mary, didn't you?'

Mary looked worried. 'Yes, in a way. But it really isn't a gift. Mildred gave me Elizabeth, you see, in exchange.'

'She has the keys of the Kingdom, as well as the key of Elizabeth's heart, Will,' said Mother, looking at Father across the breakfast table.

'What does that mean,' Stephen solemnly inquired, digging a spoon into his porridge.

'It means different things to different people,' said Mother, 'but to me it means the gift of being able to distinguish between the real and the false.' Then, knowing the children could not understand such grown-up talk, she added, 'It means knowing whether what you are choosing is a diamond or an ordinary stone.'

From her cot Elizabeth suddenly wailed a warning that all was not well with her.

Mildred shouted with joy, letting the purse dangle over her arm, and chanting, while Mary lifted up her charge:

> *Goodbye, Elizabeth, goodbye;*
> *My purse is false, but does not cry!*
> *For you, O howler, I'll not sigh;*
> *Goodbye, Elizabeth, goodbye!*

Everybody laughed, and Mildred with her handsome, sparkling face, held the attention of all except Elizabeth, who scowled at her from the safety of Mary's arms.

Ten

A Map is an Exciting Thing

FROM her desk Mary looked at the big map of Australia on the green wall of the classroom and without hesitation began to draw it in miniature on the clear, white page of her drawing book. She loved to draw anything she saw, and at home, in a secret drawer, Mother kept a pile of drawing-books containing Mary's sketches of castles, cottages, gardens and flowers. Mildred could draw imposing pictures of rather hazy forests, but Mary's single tree and every tiny leaf were nearly perfect. But more than all she liked to draw maps.

The map showed the five states of Australia: egg coloured for the North; green for the South; grey for Queensland; yellow for New South Wales; orange for Victoria. Mary printed neatly and carefully, marking with precision rivers and mountains, inland towns and seaports.

But though her pen drew a long, wavering line and her lips were pursed up as she wrote in the name, her mind was far away. Sometimes she had wished she could live always in one place, as her grandmother and grandfather lived in Adelaide, instead of travelling from one town or city to another. Already she had memories of many houses, long train journeys and voyages around the Australian coast from Adelaide to Sydney and Brisbane or even further.

But, she reflected now, if she had not travelled, what a dull thing this map would be! The line she now drew would have been just ink on paper as it was to her physical eyes; instead, it was a long stretch of water underneath a graceful bridge. And she with Mildred, Stephen and Sheila were standing with their noses pressed against the glass windows, chanting:

Here I go;
Here I go;
Here I go to Timbuktu

keeping time with the rhythm of the wheels. When she shaded a long, narrow strip she saw in her mind the Australian Alps, and an orange speeding from Father's hand through the train's open window like an escaped cricket ball, while an Aborigine came running through the trees to catch it. Sometimes as, with crayon, she shaded the five states she saw wheat fields bowing in the sunshine and sheep grazing on green grass, or smelled fresh breezes from the eucalyptus forests. Sometimes she saw a bush dweller walking toward the sunset swinging his billy-can, or trees bowed with their golden burden of wattle.

Often the pictures in her mind were not beautiful. M-O-O-N-T-A, she printed, and saw a mine shaft and, not far away, cottages of wattle and daub, the big men with dirty faces listening while her father told them how sad it would be if, while they searched for wealth, they neglected to seek God. Once a boiler had burst at the top of a mine and many men had been killed. Mary remembered her mother's sadness. At such times the first question was always, 'Were the men converted? Did they know God?'

As Mary measured the spot where Broken Hill must be printed in New South Wales, she 'saw' a great open-air meeting, past which mounted troopers guided their splendid horses with seeming carelessness, yet watchfully guarding every movement of the people lest new riots between miners and free labourers should startle the town. In Broken Hill people talked of the 'White Queen' who had lured thousands of men to her side and ruined and robbed them. The 'White Queen' was the silver in the mines, and the ruined men were the strikers whose wealth had been so short-lived and whose families were suffering in consequence. Sometimes, Father explained, wealth, in the hands of those who did not know how to us it wisely, caused greater misery than poverty. Many of those who served the 'White Queen' drank and gambled and never thought of God.

To Mary, every city, village, forest, field, desert or mountain was a place peopled by men and women, boys and girls for whom her father and mother toiled, prayed and lived that they might be led to God.

Mary spent much time over her map, and when she had finished drawing and writing, the teacher pinned it on the blackboard for all to see; then she let Mary have it to take home. With her mother she talked about the places on the map to which they had been and how she had thought of their travels while she worked.

'Drawing a map of a country you haven't seen,' said Mother, 'is like hearing about God but not knowing him. Or, like looking at the outside of a house but not having the key to let yourself in.'

Mary felt she knew a great deal about God. But, she pondered, did she know him?

This question was still unanswered when Father told her he was going to Melbourne where a commissioner, once a railway guard in faraway England, was going to conduct meetings.

James Dowdle, Father said, was feeling the intense heat of Australia after the moderate climate of England, but in his meetings many people were being led to God.

'Mother can't come with me,' Father said to Mary. 'Would you like to keep me company?'

Underneath her quiet manner, Mary's happiness made her tremble. It shone in her big eyes till they looked like 'seas mingled with fire'.

'Oh, I would,' she said.

As soon as Mary and Captain Angus reached Melbourne, Salvationists seemed to appear from all quarters to speak to her father. Always they asked how the work was progressing – were men and women coming to God? Sadness or happiness depended on the answer to this question.

Father seemed to know everybody, and everybody seemed to be glad to talk with him. Mary felt small among so many grown-ups, but Father held her hand and she knew she was safe.

The converted railway guard had a fiddle which he used in an officers' meeting to accompany the singing of:

> Soldiers fighting round the Cross,
> Fight for your Lord;
> Reckon all things else but loss,
> Fight for your Lord.

When the audience began to sing the last line, he jerked up the bow vigorously as if it were a sword cutting down 'losses'. Sometimes he waved it about like a baton, joyously.

At night, James Dowdle preached about the awfulness of sin and of how it shut men away from the God who made them for himself.

Already Mary had seen what sin could do to men and women. Sin made the miners spend their money to buy beer, and gamble it away till they sometimes lost all their possessions. Sin made mine owners do unkind, even cruel acts. She had seen what bitterness men of one race can show to men of another. That was why a Chinese convert was treated with particular gentleness by Father and

Mother. And she had seen in Australia that fear of one another made men of different nationalities hate and try to hurt each other.

She had seen, too, how God casts out sin and makes employees and employers give and take, each seeking to do the other justice. She had seen in the Army march rich and poor, educated and ignorant all working together.

Poll Cot often came to see Mary's mother. Poll had once been the terror of Sydney shopkeepers, beating about the head those who would not serve her. She had often been imprisoned and the police dreaded their task of arresting her, for she could fight six at a time. Now she was so gentle that the Angus children greeted news of a visit from her as a happy event.

James Dowdle said that sin separated men from God. He painted a terrible picture of what such a separation from the source of all goodness would be like, and then he told the people that only One could save them and that One was Jesus.

Men and women came to the penitent form. Mary listened to the tramp, tramp of their feet as they went forward until there were three rows, one behind the other. Mary had not left her father's side all day, but she left him now, walking quietly, shyly along the aisle that seemed a mile long. No one, except Father, noticed the slight figure of a child kneeling, hidden behind the grown-ups, praying. Mary was not aware of sin or of desire to do anything but good. Had he known she was there, James Dowdle might have been thinking of her when he brought down the bow of his fiddle and began to lead the crowd in singing,

> *I heard the voice of Jesus say:*
> *I am this dark world's Light;*
> *Look unto me, thy morn shall rise,*
> *And all thy day be bright.*

Among those who had gravely sinned and strayed far into the darkness of being apart from God, Mary knelt. She knew Jesus was their Light; but he was also the Light for a child starting on life's way. She knew that for her the 'morn had risen'. In Jesus she had the key her mother had talked about – the key to the Kingdom of God. Now she would always know how to choose the best.

Mary would soon be back at school, perhaps drawing another map, marking the dot that is Melbourne and seeing a new, beautiful, exciting scene in which, for once, she was the central figure.

Eleven

A Farthing for a Day's Work

'SELF-DENIAL WEEK begins tomorrow,' Mary announced, piling her books on the table ready to commence homework. She sounded excited, as she did when the family set out on a journey.

'Now what has Self-Denial to do with my arithmetic?' demanded Mildred, opening a red book and propping it against the lamp.

Mary laughed. 'Maybe we'll have to do some arithmetic before we smash our targets.' she said. What's yours?'

'Two shillings,' said Mildred shortly.

'Mine's three shillings,' said Mary. 'That's a lot, isn't it?'

'Mm,' said Mildred disinterestedly, and began to write 'Arithmetic' in curly letters at the top of a new, white page in her exercise book. Soon she had forgotten all around. Mary was writing, too, but while she worked at subtraction and addition of money, she thought of her father's treasure box.

In the box on a poster, yellow and torn with age, were the words:

TOWARD THE INVASION OF CHINA

When the poster had first been printed people had crowded around it as they often crowded at newspaper stands in times of crises, for at that time Australians still talked of the days when miners had objected to men of another country coming to work in the goldfields of New South Wales. Nearly 30 years before there had been riots; and in 1888 a conference had been held in Sydney with delegates from all the states to discuss a situation which had appeared to be a menace. In 1886 any word about the Chinese and China had demanded attention, and Salvationists, not concerned with party politics, had used every means of attracting the notice of people so that they might tell them about God.

But Australians had not been the only ones who stared in astonishment at the bill. The attention of the Chinese had been arrested. Surely Australia would not declare war against China, they had thought. The peace-loving Chinese were as startled as their Australian friends. Most of the Chinese who had remained in Australia sold vegetables grown by themselves; some kept little shops. Generally they were successful for they did not drink and they were hard working, gaining the usual results of industriousness.

But they had discovered the bill was not an announcement of the landing of military forces in China but that an Army equipped not with guns but with the love and grace of God was about to march the streets of Sydney's Chinatown.

Attached to the bill announcing the 'invasion' was another in Chinese characters which Mary thought beautiful. This one gave the news that on Sunday 4 January 1886 a meeting would be held in the No 3 Barracks, Waterloo Junction. Sergeant Lung Fue would invite all his friends to be there.

That had happened a long time ago but Mary was always interested in China and the Chinese. She was interested because of Moy Sam who kept a shop not far from the Army quarters where Elizabeth was born.

Moy Sam welcomed all the Anguses to his home and they liked to be there among the scent of spices mingled with the aroma of roasting pork and candied sweet potatoes. They liked to help wash the rice about which Mrs Moy was so particular.

If a junior soldier was able to raise money for the Self-Denial effort The Salvation Army would be able to send officers to more and more countries, reasoned Mary. They would one day be able to invade not only the China in Sydney but the real China, which must be a wonderful land if all the people there were like Moy Sam. Mother said that one always judges a distant country by its best, not its worst, representatives.

That China might be inhabited by men like those in the opium dens behind the quarters never occurred to Mary. The Chinese people she knew were clean and kind. Sometimes they came to the door with vegetables in two huge baskets suspended from a strong bamboo that lay across their shoulders. They wore big hats, baggy blue trousers and loose coats, and they trotted along as though the laden baskets were filled with feathers. One Chinese man with a long, thick, shiny, black pigtail marched behind the drum every Saturday night, and gave his testimony, telling how he now believed in Jesus, the true Way.

Mary knew why Salvationists had a Self-Denial Week, for Father had told her how the Founder had once talked to a crowd of people in Exeter Hall, England, and how they had written their names on a yellow form called a 'canary' and promised sums of money to extend the work. One 'canary' had been signed 'John Carleton' and had read: 'By going without pudding every day for one year, I calculate I shall save 50 shillings. This I will do, and will remit the amount named as soon as possible.'

William Booth had felt that to ask every Salvationist to deny himself in this way for a year might be too much. But all could be asked to take part in a week's effort. Soon the word had been passed to every land where the Army was at work and cheerfully accepted everywhere. Mary began to divide 50 shillings by 365 to find out how much John Carleton's pudding cost per day.

When she and Mildred had finished their homework Mary asked her mother if she could give up the rice pudding they all had at dinner nearly every day. But Mrs Angus had another plan. In the kitchen, with Elizabeth on her lap and the four older children listening, she unfolded it, speaking to the children in a reasonable manner, as Father spoke to the soldiers in a meeting held specially for them on Tuesday nights.

She said that to give up food needed to keep them well would be wrong. God wanted everybody to look after the body so they could work well. What they could do, if they agreed to the plan, was to give up luxuries. At the end of the week, Mother said, she would divide between them, according to the size of each target, all she had saved on the grocery bill.

She asked them to tell her what they chose to be without during Self-Denial Week. Butter, then sixpence a pound, was first on the list. The older children who drank tea offered to go without sugar. Even Sheila wanted to eat her porridge without milk. No one would eat sweets or cakes. Mary felt she was launching on an exciting adventure. But she thought she ought to do more. On Saturday morning she was up early bringing in the wood and washing the dishes, so she could begin collecting as soon as the shops opened.

Collecting money, even with people like Moy Sam in mind, was not easy for Mary. As she knocked at every door her heart thumped. In every shop her face burned with shyness. No one seemed to have any money to give. Sometimes women slammed their doors in Mary's face, but she made up her mind that, like every other job, collecting had to be done thoroughly. Her feet ached; her head ached; her cheeks were so pale that her big eyes appeared black, but she never missed a house. At the end of the last street she examined her card ruefully. On the card was painted a target with 6d, 3d, 1d, 1/2d, 1/4d marked on it. If anyone gave, he was asked to prick the amount. For a whole day's walking and asking, Mary's card showed one prick and that was over the farthing sign.

She must not go in the streets behind the quarters, Mother had said, for there men shuffled into dark, dusty rooms, and drunken men fought each other for no particular reason. She must go home now, for after tea Mother would be at the meeting and she would be sitting up to see that all was well while the younger children slept. Mildred was beginning to oppose her sister's orders, but Stephen, already an intelligent, capable, reliable boy, was always an ally. He was, thought Mary, like the house built in the rock in the Bible story.

From the ill-kept homes nearby, rats found their way into the quarters – huge, long-tailed creatures so bold that, if she did not want them to tumble over her feet, she had to rattle the door-knob loudly before she opened it. Perhaps the rats would have a quiet night, she thought, as she went through the door scarcely able to lift her aching feet.

'I've only collected a farthing,' she said to Mother.

'Never mind,' said Mother. 'What do you think I've saved on the grocery bill?'

Mary couldn't guess.

'Six shillings,' said Mrs. Angus. 'And because you have the highest target and have given up so much, you shall have two.' She took Mary's card and pricked twelve of the 1d marks and two 6d marks. 'We'll leave the farthings for another day.'

'Guess what!' went on Mother. 'Moy Sam has asked us to dinner on the day after Self-Denial.' Mary wondered if John Carleton in England had known anyone like Moy Sam. She wondered about England where the weather was cold and grey in the Self-Denial season. But she could not know that, in Canning Town, England, a young man was staring at a Self-Denial envelope and wishing he had more to put in it.

Twelve

A Soldier in the Home

MARY was a soldier. Since the day she had knelt among the men and women at the penitent form praying that Jesus Christ would be her Saviour and Guide, she, though gentle and quiet, had been a dynamic person with definite ideas about right and wrong. No girl who sat next to Mary in the school classroom found it easy to be dishonest, unkind or even untidy. Long before she was old enough to be sworn-in as a Salvation Army soldier she was doing what The Salvation Army expects soldiers to do.

School, homework, housework and looking after Elizabeth kept Mary busy. Often, at night, her feet ached so that she could scarcely bear her shoes. But to Father or Mother she never mentioned weariness. Even Elizabeth, never far from her, could not guess how tired Mary was when bedtime came.

Mary regarded the younger members of the family as her responsibility. Home was a fine battleground for a soldier. From the beginning, children had to be shown the right way to perform the smallest household task. 'Not to know how to cook and clean would be a disgrace,' Mary said, 'even if you were a princess.' Under Mary's direction scrubbing a floor became an adventure. Sheila and Stephen were her best pupils. By the time Stephen was 13, Mrs Angus said, he could scrub a floor and polish the silver more efficiently than any girl.

Mary's rules were few: the hidden corners were more important than the seen spaces; after the scrubbing, all soap must be rinsed off and the final wiping should leave the linoleum nearly dry. When work was done, a word of praise from Mary was more valuable than a whole speech from someone less particular.

Elizabeth was a frail child, not allowed to do more than clear up the yard, which she did somewhat carelessly, thinking more of the weekly penny she was given for doing it than of a neat yard.

'The yard isn't clear until you've picked up every single scrap of paper or rubbish, Elizabeth,' Mary said firmly. 'You ought to be ashamed to take a penny from Mother this week.' Elizabeth was ashamed, after Mary's eyes had bored into her. And she went into the yard again, carefully gathering up all the rubbish she could find.

As Elizabeth was not yet strong enough to go to school, Mary decided she should not be denied the joy of learning. While she washed dishes and baked, she taught Elizabeth to say the alphabet backwards and forwards. She was never too tired or too busy to explain the meaning of a word. Even on washing days when, among sheets and blankets, 16 white pinafores hung on the line, Mary worked with

Mother until it was time to go to school. She was never impatient with Elizabeth who, book in hand, followed her with questions.

'I want Mary to dress me,' Elizabeth would wail if anyone else tried to help her with tapes and buttons. And Mary would come, rather pleased, and tempted to give in because of the compliment of being preferred. 'But you are nearly five now,' she said one day. Wouldn't it be nice to learn how to dress yourself? Then when I'm not here you'll manage alone.'

Not here! Elizabeth's eyes opened, wide and frightened. A house without Mary would, for her, be a cold and dark place.

'Are you going away?' she asked nervously.

'No,' said Mary hastily. 'I meant when I'm at school.'

That was bad enough. Every afternoon Elizabeth sat moping in a corner, waiting for the hour when she could rush out and meet Mary.

Mary did not approve of Elizabeth's moping in her absence, or of the worry she caused Mother by scarcely eating. Mary said these things were wrong because they made other people unhappy, and making other people sad is selfish. Elizabeth was troubled. She had never known Mary to think first of self, but she said, 'I don't know how not to be selfish.'

Mary persuaded her to ask God to help her to think of others.

'Do you mean at the penitent form in the juniors on Sunday?' the little girl asked.

'Oh no,' said Mary. 'When you know you are wrong, you don't wait for any day or place, you kneel down wherever you are. You can ask God now to make you good.'

She brought out an old wooden chair and, in the centre of the kitchen floor, Elizabeth knelt to pray. For the first time in her life she felt a need of being forgiven.

One day a friend gave Elizabeth the most beautiful doll she had ever had, with a kid-leather body and a lovely china head, with real hair that could be combed and plaited. The doll, named Nancy, was dressed in a blue Salvation Army uniform, with a tiny bonnet, perfect even to the red band with 'The Salvation Army' embroidered on it.

'Oh,' said Elizabeth in delight, 'just like Mother.'

'No, not a bit like Mother,' said Mary. 'She wears uniform because it says to the people that she loves God and is his servant and theirs, when they need her. A doll ought not to be in uniform.'

She did not remove the uniform at once. But one morning Elizabeth awoke to find beside her bed a whole set of doll's clothes, imitations of her own garments. There was a neat printed dress, with a yoke, tiny cuffs and the smallest button holes she had ever seen. Sitting up in bed, Elizabeth carefully removed Nancy's uniform and gave it to Mary to put away. She spent nearly the whole of that day dressing and undressing Nancy.

Mary loved school, but Father, as a divisional officer, was very busy and Mother seemed always to be working. Her face, becoming white and very thin, troubled Mary, so one day she decided to solve the problem of how best to be of use. Mary never tried to evade her problem, for that was not her way. She knelt beside the bed in her tiny bedroom off the big veranda. In the silence, always remembering that Christ was her Light, she waited and thought.

Father and Mother could not afford to have paid help; Mother would be ill if she did not have more help, and without her Father could not carry on; Mary could not do any more than she was already doing. Already by early afternoon she was too tired to concentrate on lessons. Therefore, the way seemed clear. She must ask Mother to let her leave school.

Mary told Elizabeth first. 'I'm not going back to school after the holiday,' she said cheerfully as she brushed the child's unruly, fine hair. 'I'm going to stay home and help Mother.'

Elizabeth stood breathless, unable to believe the news. 'Then, you'll be here all the time, Mary?'

'Yes. Shall you be glad?'

'Oh, Mary!' Elizabeth could not say more. Now would the warm, clear light always be shining where she was. She had no words to express what was in her, but Mary knew.

Around the dining-room table Stephen, Sheila and Mildred did their homework. Waving her ruler, Mildred pointed to the candles on the piano where Mary had lately been practising. 'Extinguish those nocturnal illuminators!' she exclaimed.

'What ails thee, far-from-fair maiden?' demanded Stephen, pointing his ruler at Mildred.

'The illustrious instructor of our academy has told us we must cultivate the art of using unusual words,' said Mildred.

'Then,' said Stephen, 'make it "dowse the glim"!'

Sheila gravely copying out and trying to learn *The Little Red Hen*, asked for another way of saying 'little red hen'.

'The minute scarlet – oh, I can't think of anything but hen, for hen,' mourned Sheila.

'I can,' shouted Mildred. 'Elizabeth!'

Their gaiety made Mary feel out of it all. Standing in the shadows near the piano she quickly glanced at Elizabeth looking for signs of hurt in her eyes and finding none she smiled. No longer was she one of this merry student party; she was only an onlooker. But a soldier does not complain, and Mary, joining in the happy hunt for words, hurried away to find Father's big dictionary. Elizabeth ran after her, not at all sure she liked being called a hen, but thinking that if Mary had not complained on her behalf it must be all right.

Thirteen

The Army for Me

'MMMMM, honeysuckle!' murmured Mrs Angus, breathing in the scented air as the cab drew up outside the wide gates of the divisional headquarters in Toowoomba, the new home of the Anguses. Mary sighed contentedly, squeezing Elizabeth's hand. Mother's ecstatic murmur meant that the appearance of the new home made her glad. Mother's wants were few. She liked clean, large rooms and a garden where she could plant flowers and where the children could play and have pets.

In the dusk Mary could see a passion fruit vine, tangerine trees and blossoming honeysuckle growing over the side of a wide veranda.

They were all tired but, as the family sat around the big kitchen table laden with good things baked by Mrs Perrett, a German neighbour who had prepared a meal, Mary had a sense of contentment. This was a friendly house, and the town would be friendly too, she believed. She had heard of the corps, for Captain William McKenzie, once her father's lieutenant, had been the commanding officer and had married Anne Hoepper, a charming member of a family of six. Her brothers Ferdie, Karl and Jack played in the fine band.

Toowoomba was the Garden City of Queensland, rich in fertile soil. Every Saturday Mrs Rathmüller, who regularly attended the meetings, drove in from a farm, bringing a huge basket of marrows, carrots, potatoes and cabbages for which she charged only sixpence, though it lasted the Angus family a whole week. Mrs Perret owned a cow, and every morning Elizabeth called for a big pitcher of warm milk for the morning porridge.

Mary was happy playing in the tambourine band, singing carols with the corps cadets, working at home harder than ever, for Mother had to enter the Brisbane hospital, and for several months Mary was both housekeeper and mother.

Mary was often troubled by what she read in the newspapers. For nearly two years the South African War had been raging. Stephen had told her how Father had taken him to the edge of the cliffs in Newcastle, not far from the big swimming pool made in a huge rock by the convicts, and how they had seen the White Star liner *Medic*, her decks crowded with soldiers, the first Australians to join the British in South Africa, sailing along the Hunter River toward the sea.

'Why did Father stand there watching?' Stephen asked. 'Unless it was because he wished he could go to South Africa to fight with the Australians and the British?'

Mary did not know. The war puzzled her. Some people said this was a war against evil. Others said that if there were no gold or diamonds in Kimberley and Johannesburg, there would be no war. Mary knew that guns could not stop evil. 'We do not shoot drunken men; we try to save them,' she reasoned. As for wanting diamonds and gold, who wanted these treasures? Father didn't, neither did Stephen's schoolmaster, who went off to Africa, leaving on the station a crowd of cheering boys. Mary was sure there were lots of Afrikaners who did not want gold, and who would like to live in peace on their farms.

Every month Father received a copy of *All the World*. He kept every copy, and from a big boxful Mary read studiously in the back numbers everything she could find about the war, though the more she read the more puzzled she became. She could not help being moved when she heard that Adjutant Mary Murray, daughter of General Sir John Murray, KCB, had gone to South Africa with a party of 10 Salvationists to do whatever The Salvation Army could do to relieve suffering. Sometimes Mary thought she would like to be with the older Mary, visiting hospitals and camps on the lonely veldt and serving hot cocoa, moving with the troops and working under shellfire. The reports said Adjutant Murray held meetings with the men and that some of them sought Christ.

Other reports described Commissioner Kilbey visiting a concentration camp where nearly 10,000 women and children were confined. Major Allister Smith had sung to them in Dutch, and the commissioner's words were translated by an interpreter.

She heard that a Dutch commandant had ministered to a sick British Salvationist and that the Zulus, a conquered race, were still a fighting race who loved to carry shields, knobkerries and assegais. Major Allister Smith said this desire to fight could be used in the service of God, and he was making Salvation Army soldiers in Zululand. This was grand, Mary thought: to have a fighting spirit and use it for overcoming evil was like Mother having a fine voice and using it to win people for God.

Despite the fact that she was British, whenever she thought of a battlefield where her wounded countrymen lay, or met a mother whose son had been killed, Mary thought of the sorrowing women on African farms and of Boers lying wounded and alone on the wide veld. The compassionate God she knew must surely be with them, as well as with the Australians and British. Mary decided that God was not on either side, but that he was calling men to be on his.

Names of towns like Ladysmith, Kimberley and Mafeking began to be as real to Mary as Toowoomba, Sydney, Goulburn, Adelaide; but, instead of seeing men kneeling at the penitent form, she now saw men lying ill with enteric, women dying in concentration camps, and men, British or Boers, firing at each other from behind the *kopjes*.

'Why doesn't God stop it all?' she heard a man ask her father; and she listened intently as he replied, 'God has given man the power to choose what he will do.'

'There will always be wars until all men are on God's side, then they will stop war. War,' said Father, 'is a symptom of a disease – like a rash is a symptom of measles.'

Light began to dawn. Mary heard that Commissioner Kilbey, travelling on horseback in Natal, had spent a night in a trappist monastery. The monks had never met a Salvationist.

'Are you of the Cape Mounted Rifles?' they asked.

'No,' said the commissioner. 'We are at war with evil.'

'Ah,' said one of the priests, 'we also are fighting the devil.'

'The whole Church of Christ,' thought Mary, 'is fighting evil.'

From a hospital in Wynberg, Corporal G. Knight had written of travelling, wounded, by ox wagon over rough roads to the hospital base. 'I love my Queen and country, and my last drop of blood should be shed in its cause if necessary. I often wonder why people, after hearing of the love of the Saviour, should not rush to give their service to him, even more than England's sons, when they know what has been done for them is far more than any Government can do.'

Mary's mind became clearer every day. She knew with certainty why her father was in The Salvation Army, waging war not against a symptom but attacking the disease called sin. He had chosen the best way of overcoming evil. No wonder he sang so lustily: 'The Salvation Army's the Army for me!' In this Army, men of all nations were united. On Sunday she looked at the flag waving at the head of the march with a new thrill.

At home she laid on the table and smoothed out a copy of the Articles of War that she had been examining for a long time. Then very slowly she signed her name. In a few weeks she would be a soldier of The Salvation Army. Some day she would become an officer. Her mind was made up:

In the kitchen with Mother next morning, she heard a loud knock. She ran to the door and, white-faced, brought back a telegram.

Mother's hands were deep in a bowl of flour, for she was making Father's special Scotch scones. 'You open it, Mary,' she said.

Mary slit the orange-coloured envelope, pulled out the message and read: 'You farewell South Africa.'

Fourteen

A Soldier Anywhere

THOUGH the war was over, Mary could scarcely think of South Africa except as a battlefield. Yet she had heard of Johannesburg, the 'golden city', and of the Kimberley diamond mines, of the deeply religious Afrikaners and of the noble Zulu and his neighbours. Her picture of the country where soon she must live was like a blur on a canvas – a blur in which she saw a battlefield, tall buildings and forests. Elizabeth's imagination went further. In fact her mental picture, not at all blurred, was clear and definite. 'We are going to live in a tent in a forest,' she announced firmly to Julian Perrett, 'and we shall have tree trunks for chairs and lions for pets.'

'You can't play with lions,' Julian pointed out, his square, boyish face puzzled, for Elizabeth, as always, seemed certain she was right. 'They just eat you when you try,' he told her.

'Ours won't be that sort,' said Elizabeth in decided tones and skipped away in her new red dress wondering why, on this exciting day when they were leaving for a land of mystery, her mother should be going from room to room looking so sad, or lingering on the veranda, burying her face in the honeysuckle.

'I expect the African forest is chock full of honeysuckle,' she said to Mary in a rather impatient voice.

Mary said that Australia had been Mother's home since she was almost as young as Elizabeth; that all her children had been born there, that she had met Father in Australia and that she was thinking of men and women, like Brother Brown, whom she and Father had led to God and might never see again.

Elizabeth thought Africa would make up for all that; so Mary said, 'Would you feel sad if you had to leave us all, without even saying goodbye? That's what Mother is having to do.'

'How?' asked Elizabeth.

'The *Persic* does not call at Adelaide, so Mother won't see Grandmother and Grandfather, or Uncle Bert and Uncle Jack, not even Aunty Amy.'

Elizabeth stopped skipping about, and walked soberly into the bedroom. She found her mother resting quietly, and she stood close to her, tracing with warm fingers the new lines in her mother's forehead.

'Are you sad at leaving Toowoomba, Mother?' she asked.

'Yes,' said Mrs Angus, 'in a way.'

'Why are you going, then?' asked Elizabeth.

'Because Father is needed in Africa, and a soldier goes where he is needed.'

'The lions will be nice to have, won't they?' said Elizabeth comfortingly.

'Oh, wonderful!' said Mother and, looking at Mary, she laughed quite gaily, just as the sound of horses' hooves was heard at the gate and Father called from the veranda steps, 'It's time to go!'

Mary gazed backward at the square house where Mrs Perrett, Julian and Louie stood, waving goodbye.

An hour later the train steamed out and the shunting sound of the engine mingled with the voices of Salvation Army soldiers standing on the platform singing:

God be with you till we meet again,
Keep love's banner floating o'er you,
Smite death's threatening wave before you;
God be with you till we meet again!

On a foggy September morning the *Persic* silently, like a ghost ship, sailed into Table Bay, South Africa. Mary and Stephen, trying to catch a glimpse of the mountains other passengers had described, saw only a wall of fog. Peering into the sea, they wondered at the clouded water and learned afterwards that the *Persic* had narrowly missed crashing against the rocks. Hours passed before the mist thinned, the sun seeming to wrestle for supremacy and quietly absorbing the veil that had hung over sea and land. Mary saw the long, straight outline of Table Mountain, then the sunlit slopes in what appeared as pale green velvet and at last rooftops nestling with the circle of mountains that towered like kindly guardians of the land. Busy tugs chugged to the side of the ship, and Mary, holding Elizabeth's hand at the foot of the ladder, waited till the swirling waters lifted the tug near enough for her to jump in and for a sailor to lift Elizabeth into her lap.

As the tug chugged its way landward, voices floated out from the pier. Mary looked at her father and mother and saw their faces pale, but smiling, as they joined the chorus:

> *So we'll lift up the banner on high,*
> *The salvation banner of love;*
> *We'll fight beneath its colours till we die,*
> *Then go to our home above.*

Not far from the pier Mary could see a Cape cart standing. A boy holding the horse's bridle grinned at her. The cart had two wheels and, when seven people were piled in it, tipped backward in an alarming manner. Sheila screamed, but the boy looked at Father and in a husky, deep voice said, It's all right, once we git goin'.'

As they jogged along Mary saw beautiful buildings which included a castle, a long road where trams, much like those in Australia and drawn by horses, clattered past lighted shops and public houses. Then they passed some small terraced houses and the boy halted the horse in front of No 2

Congregational Terrace. They were home. A Salvation Army officer with a rosy face opened the door and told them that when they were ready they were to come next door where tea awaited them.

'There aren't any lions,' mourned Elizabeth. 'We might as well have stayed in Australia.'

'We didn't come here to play with lions,' Mary said. 'We're soldiers, consecrated to the unexpected.' Of course she didn't imagine Elizabeth would know what she meant, but Elizabeth knew she had been rebuked.

As she went about the house during the next few weeks, taking over more and more of washing, ironing and scrubbing, becoming more active at the Cape Town Citadel Corps, she reflected that she was doing nothing different from what she had done in Australia, except that she had left friends and all familiar things behind. Now instead of hanging white pinafores in a big open yard scented with honeysuckle she hung them on a line slung from wall to wall of a narrow asphalted square, the door of which opened into a dusty lane. Even while she reflected she heard the rumble of cartwheels and a raucous voice shouting, 'Snoek, snoek, snoek – any snoek, any snoek, snooooek?'

The smell of fish for the scent of blossoms was her portion.

But Mary was a soldier in God's Army. She remembered the letter in *All the World*: 'I often wonder why people, after hearing of the love of the

Saviour, should not rush to give their service to him, more than England's sons, when they know what has been done for them.'

She would serve God anywhere, even at a wash-tub. As she rubbed, her lips tightened in determination.

Fifteen

Mary Sees the Mountains Again

SHEILA sat on the back steps making up a song which she sang as she dolefully rocked herself backwards and forwards:

> *For it's don't do this and don't do that,*
> *And I never told you to do that,*
> *And that's not right, and this is wrong*
> *When mothers are in bed.*

Elizabeth joined her, quickly learning the made-up words and tune and, in the back yard, the two youngest members of the Angus family loudly duetted till they drowned even the cry of the fishmonger. They sang for the benefit of the older members of the household from whom they had to take orders while Mother was ill. But when Mary came out from where she had been ironing, and hung the clean sheets in the sun to air, Elizabeth took a long look at her face, and ceased to sing. Never before had Mary looked so sad and weary.

In the weeks that followed, Stephen, always practical, said that if a girl could do housework, so could a boy. A boy, he said, could even cook if he followed the directions given in the cookery book.

Stephen had not yet started work at the General Post Office where he had secured a position, so he and Mother had a conference. Mildred was already at a business college. Mary had seen an advertisement for an accountant with a good handwriting and everybody knew how neat and beautiful were Mary's figures, printing and writing. But though she longed to take the position, she thought she could not leave home.

Stephen solved her problem, and for many months he took her place. The sound of his scrubbing brush echoed through the sparsely furnished rooms, and even Mary, so particular, could find no speck of dust anywhere. The whole house shone. He was a born teacher, too, and Elizabeth, still considered too delicate for school, learned from him how to subtract and to multiply. Though she had been slow learning to read, by the time she was eight a sixth form book was not too difficult. She devoured every book she could lay hands on. Mary and Mother saw that only good books lay within her reach.

At Cape Town Citadel Corps the family were now at home. They had new friends, and Elizabeth often heard them talking of Agnes and Arthur Pearce, of Katie and Allister Smith, Catherine Esplin and, later, of Margaret and Herbert Richards and other young enthusiastic Salvationists. Mary, by her own efforts, had emerged in spirit from the small, square, asphalt yard to the beautiful broad streets from which she could look upwards to the shining silver leaves on the slopes of Table Mountain. She proudly gave her earnings to Mrs Angus every week, keeping only enough for cartridges and lunches. Clever Mildred had passed through the business college and was at work in a lawyer's office. Her salary helped to pay school fees for Sheila at Wynberg High School.

It now seemed that Africa was as rich in beauty and friendship as Australia, but Mary was not satisfied with merely enjoying beauty and friendship. Once she had gone into that part of Cape Town known as District Six. Along cobble-stone streets she had walked with a band of Salvation Army soldiers. She had seen sailors reeling from the public houses, drunk, cursing, using language that made her shudder. She had seen girls no older than herself, earning 15 shillings a week, living with five others in one room supporting their families. A high percentage of the population had tuberculosis, an equally high percentage suffered from more dreadful diseases resulting from sin. Men and boys stood around the little ring of Salvationists, blaspheming whenever the name of Jesus was mentioned.

'Don't think of that awful part of Cape Town,' said Mary's companions at the office; 'think only of the grandeur of the mountains towering above District Six.'

Mary replied, 'When I look at District Six I cannot see the mountains. Beauty is meant only for those who have done their best to put an end to sin and squalor.'

Mary knew she must be a candidate now. There was no other way.

Her candidateship did not last long. Commissioner Richards, the Territorial Commander, and Colonel Pearce, the Chief Secretary, were soldiers at Mary's corps and they had noticed the quiet girl with the dynamic qualities. They had marked her steady work and her quick decisions for right. One day she received a letter asking her if, while waiting to enter the training college in Claremont, she would be willing to assist at a corps.

Mary showed the letter to Mother, to Mildred and to Stephen; none of them knew whether the corps would be near home or over the mountains to a town several days' journey away from the Cape. But Mary had no doubts about what she should do, for before anyone else had seen her message from headquarters she had quickly counted the cost, not for herself, but for her mother and brother, asking that God would help her to do enough for him to justify the sacrifice her mother would make through the departure of her firstborn.

Across the dining-room table she looked at Mrs Angus. 'Mother, Stephen will always help you. Do you mind my going?'

Mrs Angus smiled. 'Mary,' she said, 'if you did not want to be an officer, it would break my heart. I shall be so proud of you.'

Elizabeth, sitting by the fire, had her nose in a book, but she was not reading; she was listening. Her world at present was peopled with boys and girls in books, the children at the small school to which she had, at last, been sent, and with the family. Mildred was a vague presence, like a princess who could wave a wand and make a table look beautiful for Christmas or a birthday, but who was not specially fond of small sisters. Stephen was one who knew everything, and who would never let anyone hurt her. Sheila was a playmate sharing her toys, her books, her secrets. But Mary was like the lamp beside the hearth. If the lamp were taken away … She raised her dark head.

'Look!' she heard Mother say. Mary turned toward Elizabeth and saw a startled, white face, a wide, set mouth, two eyes, dark with grief, staring at them both.

'What is the matter, Elizabeth?' Mary asked gently. Elizabeth could not say. Her eyes were fixed as though nothing could ever move them again.

'I think it's time you were in bed,' Mrs Angus said.

Elizabeth, accustomed to prompt obedience, put down her book and got up as if she were dreaming. She stumbled toward Mary and slipped an ice-cold hand into her sister's warm one.

When she was tucked in bed, Mary said, 'You'll be able to come to the tram and see me off, all by yourself.' Mary knew Elizabeth liked wandering alone over the veld. She knew, too, that Elizabeth never cried now, and that a child feels many things, but knows not the words with which to tell them. Mary did not expect an answer, so she went on: 'And when I am working in my corps, you'll be able to visit me, and come with me to the open-air meeting.' No answer came. Only two eyes stared blankly into the face that had first brought comfort to their owner.

Mary remained sitting on the bed holding Elizabeth's cold hand until it was warm, until the fingers relaxed and the sorrowful eyes closed in sleep. When the postman knocked the following morning the child still slept. There was one letter for Mary, from the Divisional Commander of the Western Division, appointing her to assist Ensign Fletcher at District Six.

Mary stared at the paper. 'Now I can look at the mountains again,' she said. 'But how can I face Elizabeth? I can never take her to a place where she will see such unhappy sights, to areas beyond police bounds. Oh, Elizabeth, how can I give you up?'

Sixteen

Commissioned

ONE evening, after Elizabeth was in bed, Father and Stephen carried Mary's trunk to the station and saw her safely into the train. Then they left her. In the morning she was to be back at home for the day, and Elizabeth, Mary had promised, should see her to a tram that ran through Observatory, along Sir Lowry Road to the city of Cape Town.

To reach the quarters Mary had to battle with what is known in South Africa as a south-easter. The wind was like an angry person who did not approve of Mary's walking along streets which even policemen avoided. Bending her slight body into the wind as if she were leaning into the waves of a furious sea, she gave up trying to keep her bonnet ribbons tied, and they lashed, now behind, now in front of her, now round her neck and chest. Tin cans and pieces of newspaper clattered along the cobblestone road, down hill or wherever the wind took them. The shutters, fastened back against the stone walls of the quarters, creaked as if strong hands were trying to wrench them from their hinges. Then the door was flung open and Mary saw Ensign Fletcher's bright black hair and equally black, flashing eyes and smile. Inside the friendly little dining-room she forgot the fury, though windows and doors rattled as if the wind were saying, 'I'll burst through and snatch you out!'

The small diningroom opened into a smaller kitchen. A flight of steep stairs led up to the two bedrooms. Mary sniffed and said 'Ah!' as she looked at uncovered floors and stairs spotlessly white. She could smell soap, the kind she had used in Toowoomba. After Mary had drunk a cup of hot tea and retied her bonnet ribbons, Ensign Fletcher took her through to the kitchen across the yard into the hall. It was small but clean, like the quarters.

Mary was not long in District Six before she found that many people had been made pure in heart by God. Those who had stolen, stole no more; those who had lied were now truthful, clean, honest in business. With Ensign Fletcher, Mary, though so young, taught her people that, because they loved God, their appearance and their homes must be unlike the neglected, dirty houses of those less fortunate than they. They had many sorrows, but never must they expect others to do for them anything they could do for themselves. They must be worthy followers of God, living so that they could respect each other.

Mary admired Brother Lakay, whose shoes shone like mirrors, whose uniform trousers had a crease as perfect as that of any Australian bandsman's. She never forgot the kindness of Sister Veldsman who mothered abandoned children, and Hester Moses whose tambourine was rarely silent in testimony meetings. Hester worked diligently in the corps where there were three senior meetings on Sunday and one every night. But what she said in her happy testimony on Sunday was proved at work in a large home for old people where she worked as cook every day all through the years.

Their goodness and enthusiasm made up to Mary for the persistent memory of Elizabeth's drooping figure as she had waved goodbye and turned from the tramline to cross the field back to Congregational Terrace. This memory never faded though Major and Mrs Angus now lived in Diep River, a more distant suburb, where there was room for Sheila and Elizabeth to enjoy the sunshine.

Every week, on Mary's free afternoon, Elizabeth rushed to meet her sister, climbing into her lap, tightly shutting her eyes and leaning against her shoulder. There she would stay until a call for tea caused Mary to move, though sometimes her legs were numb from Elizabeth's weight, and they laughed together over the 'pins and needles'.

Father and Mother were proud of Mary, and of Mildred, only 17 but also a cadet. Stephen was proud, too, and, because the call that had come to Mary and her sister meant Sheila's school fees had to be paid out of a meagre salary, he gave Mrs Angus all his earnings. More and more Mother relied on Stephen, now much taller than herself.

One day in the Cape Town Citadel, Mary and Mildred were commissioned as officers by Commissioner William Richards. Sitting on the platform, waiting to be called and learn the name of the town to which she would be appointed, Mary's heart beat fast. She looked over the audience, seeing the faces of the people who had become her friends. Major and Mrs Angus and Stephen were sitting very straight, and Mary seemed to see beyond the hall, around the mountains to the tiny sitting-room where Sheila and Elizabeth were waiting, thinking of her and Mildred. Mildred's name was called first: 'Cadet Mildred Angus to be Probationary-Lieutenant, Secretary to the Chief Secretary's office at National Headquarters.'

Mary's hand trembled and everything seemed to stop until she heard:

'Cadet Mary Angus to be Probationary-Captain in charge of Port Elizabeth II.'

As she made her way back to Claremont and the training college Mary did not know that Father, Mother and Stephen were talking solemnly of the great honour that had come to her. Port Elizabeth II was, at that time, one of the hardest corps in the country. Some people would consider it anything but an honour to be sent there.

'In charge of Port Elizabeth, and only 19,' Stephen said. 'She'll do it, though.'

'The real test of courage and faith is to endure hardness over a long period. I think Mary has passed that test,' Mother said.

'How far from Cape Town is Port Elizabeth?' faltered Elizabeth.

'It takes the train about two days to get there,' said Sheila, 'and Mary'll have to sleep on the train – whizzing through the dark in the night for miles and miles, hundreds of miles.'

Stephen looked at Elizabeth's frightened face. She pressed her hand into his square, hard palm and, when she said her rather long prayer that night, Stephen was first on the list.

Mary was kneeling by the bed in a narrow cubicle at the training college, thanking God for letting her be a Salvation Army officer and praying that he would make her worthy and able to do his work in his way.

Seventeen

Mary Meets Walter

CAPTAIN MARY ANGUS, carrying Father's old Gladstone bag, alighted from the mail train with her lieutenant, a small fair-haired girl with bright eyes and a big smile. Mary glanced almost shyly up and down the platform, but no one had come to meet them, and the long train with 'C. G. R.' marked on its coaches, seemed to say, 'I am sorry, after we've travelled so far.'

But Mary had only one small trunk, and Lieutenant had no luggage at all. They could not afford a cab, they decided, so the light tin trunk was carried between them until a young man, suddenly seeing the fair lieutenant, rushed to their aid.

'Thank you,' said Mary gravely. 'If you will help us to a tram, we shall find our way.' Her steady eyes did not dance like the lieutenant's, and the young man who had hoped for some fun, found himself under Mary's orders, and doing no more and no less than she asked.

Outside the door of the railway station, Mary, smelling the sea, looked around at the beautiful buildings in the harbour area and, squeezing her lieutenant's arm, said, 'This is our town now!'

The young man escorted them on the tram. He seemed to want to come with them, but Mary firmly bid him 'Good morning!' Soon they were travelling along the one main street that ran from south to north of the city where the Port Elizabeth II hall was. On their left the streets and houses sloped upward on a high hill. Some streets were just steps with an iron rail along the side. Mary was soon to discover that, like Cape Town, Port Elizabeth was a windy city and the railings were often useful, especially when, after rainstorms, water, inches deep, swept down the asphalt paths into the main road.

North End was flat country with fewer shops. After looking over the hall, Mary said she felt as flat as the ground. As a cure for her feelings she set to scrubbing and paint washing until the dingy place was bright.

The soldiers' roll was carefully examined. Many names had been crossed off, and beside others someone had placed a question mark. Mary copied the address of a family of five into her notebook.

'The first job after the welcome meeting,' she said, 'will be visitation of all the people who haven't attended meetings lately.'

The welcome meeting was rather cool. The audience consisted of four girls and an officer from the Army's home nearby.

Mary decided to postpone visitation. She spent a whole day neatly printing cards inviting the people of North End to come to the meeting on Sunday at

11 o'clock and again at seven in the evening. On the following day the cards were distributed. On Sunday the hall was half filled. Mary, small and earnest, preached the good news that Christ was in North End with power to overcome evil. Would her listeners reach out and avail themselves of the power? Her sermon lasted only 10 minutes, but every word was like a live coal. Among the crowd was a tall, fair man wearing the dress of an Anglican clergyman. At the close of the meeting he came to Mary and, clasping her hand, said, 'Thank you, thank you. I came to the Army hall this morning because I wanted to see what the woman was like who could so meticulously print cards of invitation which I gathered must have gone to hundreds of people. I wondered if her interpretation of the gospel would match her printing. I find it does. God bless your work, and all the people who come to hear you!'

On the following Sunday the hall was full.

Captain Mary knew that crowded halls don't 'just happen'. She knew, too, that for a Salvation Army officer even a well-prepared sermon was not enough. This was her town. She must know everybody and they must know she was with them in their joys and sorrows.

At nine o'clock next morning she was knocking at the door of Mrs Brown, the woman with four daughters, against whose name the question mark had appeared. Mrs Brown looked into the young face before her, and hesitated; then she decided that in that face nothing but love and desire for her good was to be found. She began quietly to tell how a woman with an evil tongue had gossiped, so that what was a great sorrow was made to appear as sin. 'So we don't go any more,' she added. 'The girls were hurt because of me, but they love the Army.'

'And the Army loves them,' Mary said. 'Don't think that one gossip is the Army. Come back and take your place.'

Mary didn't say any more, for she was young, and Mrs Brown, old enough to be her mother, had sorrows which Mary had never experienced. But she visited the woman every week, and at last mother and daughters came back to be the nucleus of a flourishing corps. Every Sunday the hall was packed. Other ministers came to hear the girl who could say so much in so short a time. Even when special visitors were at the Citadel Corps at the other end of the city, Mary's congregations never dwindled.

No one had met her when she arrived, but when she left to be Side Officer at the training college, a crowd of soldiers stood around her singing sturdily:

I'll be true! I'll be true!
True to my Saviour in the Army.

Mary looked at the Browns and knew their feet were now too firmly on the rock for a gossip's wordy missiles to do more than sting.

The men cadets, with their Side Officer, were always lined up in the lecture hall when the women filed in. On this first morning Mary, rather shy in a new appointment for which she felt as yet unfitted, but holding her head high, walked ahead of 15 young women. As she came through the door her large eyes met those of Captain Walter Henry, standing at attention, not more than two inches taller than Mary, spick and span from his shining boots and well-brushed uniform to his thick, fair hair. Mary's heart turned a somersault and her eyes wavered. So did Walter's. He did not know that she was once the little Australian girl who after a day's collecting for Self-Denial had come wearily home with a farthing. She did not know that he had stared at a Self-Denial envelope and wished he had more to give.

Still Mary would not submit to the wavering of her own eyes. She had no intention of letting any man disturb her or take her mind from her work. She took her place on the platform calmly.

Eighteen

Where Did Walter Come From?

'WALTER!' a deep, businesslike voice called. Walter, rolled in blankets and fast asleep, heard the voice in his dream. In fact it fitted in with a dream that he was being called to the headmaster's desk for arriving late at school. But that voice had called him every morning for two years, and his mind obeyed it now. His sleepy eyes slowly opened and, while he unrolled himself from amid the blankets, he said, cheerfully, 'Righto, Dad!'

As the room was still dark, he lit a candle and held it near the alarm clock. The hands pointed to 3.30, and he must be out of the house by 4.30; he had a lot to do in a short time.

But, though he was only 10, Walter was methodical. Shivering, he stood at the sink in his pyjama trousers, vigorously washing to the waist. Then, after hurried dressing, he ate the breakfast his mother set before him, and went into the yard where Barney was waiting to be harnessed to the shafts of the coffee stall.

Fog, yellow and cold, clouded the stable and seemed to send cold, wet fingers down Walter's back. While he backed Barney into the shafts, talking to her in the same crisp voice his father used, he thought of the men, rising like himself early to work. From the yard he could generally see lights appearing in windows and know that docker Joe or Bill, as the case might be, was getting ready to dive towards the corner of Alice Street and Victoria Dock Road (London, England) for a snack before dashing for the train.

But this morning the fog was too thick for lights to show and, sitting on the shafts, Walter had to let Barney draw the coffee stall carefully along Alice Street toward the church beside which the coffee stall was always stationed. He had pulled down the counter, and was lighting the fire as his father came running along the street. This was the signal for Walter to hurry into the back door of the public house and gather up empty coffee cups left there the night before by men coming cold from work. Every night they came, looking like huge cockroaches, speeding over the bridge and down the station steps, calling for a ha'porth of coffee in a big mug which afterward, in the pub, was filled up with rum. There the men left their mugs and went home, often to comfortless houses.

It was funny, Walter thought, looking at the grey walls of the church against which his father's coffee stall stood, that in the long Dock Road there was only one church and – well he couldn't remember the names of all the public houses; there were so many.

Walter's father said one church was mightier than a thousand pubs. Walter didn't understand that, and he hadn't much time to think, for here were the men emerging from amid the fog, some pulling on their coats as they ran calling, 'Coffee in five and make it quick, mate.' To that order Walter's father would set out five saucers in a row on the clean counter and one large cup of steaming coffee, price a farthing, was poured into them. A man would drink from the saucers, buy an apple slice or a bun and rush off munching, taking the steps two at a time over the bridge to the mysterious river which somewhere spread out towards the sea.

After more than two hours' work Walter was no longer cold; perspiration trickled down his fine skin; his fair hair lay damp on his wide forehead. His blue eyes were weary.

'That'll do, boy!' he heard his father say; and like a shot he was off to school. All too often he was late, taking the punishment for lateness as part of life. Besides, Walter liked the coffee stall; he liked the men who came out to work in the cold and he liked the 'big' feeling of doing something to make them comfortable. He liked Victoria Dock Road, especially the part known as the Marsh, alive with people nearly every day in the week, buying from the stalls. Walter walked about watching men bargain, even cheat, women haggle and fuss. He talked to everybody, and none took offence at his questions, or jokes. At the coffee stall he learned the importance of cleanliness and strict honesty, and he enjoyed the increasing 'takings' of the day. Money was important,

Walter thought. With money his father bought more coffee-stalls, and later on shops and houses.

At school Walter was sleepy before lunch time, but a sleepy Walter was often quicker at his lessons than a wide-awake but lazy boy who had rolled out of his blankets at eight o'clock instead of four.

Walter had many pleasures, ranging from roaming in the busy market to playing football, and making faces at some men who had taken a dislike to boys and firing pellets at them from a gun while they streaked across the field. But there was a pleasure beyond all others: the one Walter knew when the Army captain and her lieutenant from the Canning Town Corps came to lunch in Alice Street. On that day Walter's face was scrubbed more rigorously and the parting in his hair carefully arranged. He moved quietly and was careful not to call his new trousers 'trahsis'. The captain, he thought, was an angel. On Sundays, in the little hall in Fox Street over whose doors the words 'Christian Mission Hall' still appeared, the captain watched him singing:

> *Dare to be a Daniel,*
> *Dare to stand alone,*
> *Dare to have a purpose firm,*
> *Dare to make it known.*

She thought young Walter was rather like a young angel. But only one other person shared this view, and that person was Walter's mother.

Nineteen

The Foreman Tips his Cap

WALTER was not an angel and, as he grew older, he did not regularly attend the Army hall in Fox Street. He had not changed his mind about the former captain. In fact he rather liked all Army captains. But he began to think that he was too big for the company meeting, and too big to shrink from the jokes he heard other youths make about Salvationists. Besides, singing even such rousing songs as one sang in the Army was not exciting enough for a boy who was his father's right-hand man at the coffee stall. Walter wore long trousers now, and he went often to the corner grocery store to tease the pretty girl behind the counter. He spent a great deal of money on cigarettes and the music hall was to him a great attraction.

But the clean, cheerful face of Walter Henry never failed to appear at the coffee stall. Morning after morning the fire burned merrily and the coffee, 'smelling a treat', was poured into shining cups and served on an immaculate counter. Walter's father had taught the boy well. He rarely disagreed with or even spoke sternly to his youngest child, though he had sacked an elder brother, Joe, and told him never to come near home or the stall again.

Joe never came in the daytime; but at night, when Walter was on duty alone, he came, thin, hungry, out of work, to ask for something to eat. Then young Walter would make such a cup of tea as only he could make, and serve his brother with as many buns and cakes as he could eat. One day, however, Walter was confronted by his angry father, waving a stick he had felt on rare occasions and did not wish now to feel on his back.

'Didn't I tell you you were not to have anything to do with Joe?' he shouted. 'If you've been feeding him, you're in for it. Have you?'

Standing very straight and looking into his father's angry eyes, Walter said, 'I have, Father.'

A baffled look mingled with the angry expression in Mr Henry's eyes. He demanded, 'Do you think I don't know how to bring sense into your brother's head? Do you think I have no reason for not feeding him? Why have you given him food?'

Walter sought about in his mind for the reason why, when his brother's face had appeared white and tired at the coffee stall, he had rushed to serve him. Yes, there was a reason. He stated it to his father simply, rather surprised that his father had not known. 'Why, Father? Because he is my brother.'

Mr Henry's arm fell to his side. The angry red of his face changed slowly to white. He looked at Walter as if the boy had suddenly become older and wiser than his father. Then he walked away murmuring, 'Your brother – and my son.'

Walter's next encounter with his father was less tense. He wanted to give up working at the coffee stall and secure work on his own.

'What do you mean, you young fathead?' asked the king of coffee stalls. 'You're doing well, aren't you?'

'Yes,' said Walter. 'But I want to do better. Didn't you start out alone?'

Mr Henry liked that answer and Walter set out to conquer the world. Perhaps he didn't realise as he toiled to earn 10 shillings a week that by mastering every job he tackled he was, in a sense, conquering the world. As a grocer's assistant, he made an art of measuring rice and sugar and of adding up figures. Every customer was anxious to be served by Walter. Later, with a well-known London tea merchant, he became the last word as a tea-taster.

Then young Walter, on the lookout for a better job, signed on as one of the hundreds of workers in a sugar refinery. Walter took his job seriously, and only during the lunch hour did he permit himself a game with the fellows – a game played behind great wooden cases labelled with a famous name, ready to be shipped to ports in all parts of the world. And, however aloof Foreman Hughes might be during working hours, he became remarkably friendly at lunch time behind the packing cases.

The defeated gamblers said that Walter Henry was a lucky cove, for he nearly always won with the dice, but he did not profit from these unfair earnings. At the end of the week, when the men queued at the pay desk, Walter would see Foreman Hughes watching him closely. Walter despised him, not because he gambled, but because he was a poor loser, a whiner and a cheat.

As he took his pay, he stepped toward the watching foreman and asked, scorn in his young voice, 'What did I win from you, Mr Hughes?'

'Ten bob,' said Hughes with a sinister grin.

'Take it,' said Walter; and, with only half his salary in his pocket he went home. He despised Hughes, but he did not despise the job which he would lose if he did not give the foreman back what he had lost. Yet somehow he hated himself for being willing, open-eyed, to let a man cheat him.

He was sick of this job, sick of everything. He started off to the nearest fish and chip shop when he heard the sound of singing coming from the old hall in Fox Street.

He went into the hall and sat just inside the door. How he had once taken this place for granted, like a comfortable armchair, a place pleasant to be in with friends who were glad to be with him. The faded flag still stood in its place near the reading desk. A crimson cloth covered the holiness table. The penitent form was scarred and old. Now all the familiar things seemed to come alive as the flowering fields take colour at sunrise. The faded flag seemed to say, 'Men and women have been wounded and even killed preaching the redeeming love of God; and because of them I am still in the old place beside the reading desk.' The stains on the table cloth seemed to be the tears of men weeping, as they renounced whatever had kept them away from God. The old penitent form seemed still to bear the weight of sorrowing men and women confessing wrongs and starting a new life.

'He feedeth on ashes,' Walter heard the captain saying. He did not know who it was that fed on ashes, but they must be foolish when there was bread to be had. Then he thought of the meetings behind the packing cases, of the sinister face of Hughes when he took winnings that were not his own. He thought of the shady music hall jokes and patter at which he had laughed. Could it be that he was feeding on ashes? Only two things in his life were worthwhile, work and people. He pictured the cold, tired dockers, rushing to him for coffee then turning into the public house; he saw gaslight shining on faces in the Marsh on late market days, tired faces, grim, courageous faces, evil faces, sad faces, laughing faces. He liked them all but his light-hearted banter could only cheer them for a moment. He could do nothing lasting for men and women unless he had God. Walter got up and walked to the penitent form.

Early on the following morning he was at work among the packing cases. One by one his mates assembled and the cranes began to swing outward from the docks, chains rattled, ropes creaked with the strain of heavy loads as cases of goods swung upward and outward and were lowered into place.

Suddenly Walter said, 'Chaps, I've given my heart to God.'

Bill Stokes took a few steps backward. Jim Giles dropped the heavy hook he was about to fasten to a huge roped box. Then, it seemed to Walter that every normal sound was drowned by roars of laughter.

Jim Giles wheeled around and, cupping his hands, yelled through them, 'Hey! Come and see a bloke what's given himself to God.'

Walter was already fitting his palms against a heavy crane when he saw Foreman Hughes rushing toward him, hand outstretched. 'Put it there, Wally,' he said. 'If you've given yourself to God, may he keep you. Never leave him.'

'No, sir,' said Walter. For the first time since he had known Hughes, he realised that even in him there was a seed of good.

'Have a smoke on it,' begged Stokes at lunchtime, after an unsuccessful attempt to persuade Walter to join the betting ring. 'No thanks,' said Walter. He had smoked his last cigarette.

At the end of the week he took his pay envelope. As he shoved it into his pocket he caught sight of Foreman Hughes, who smiled at the young workman, tipping his cap as he did so.

Twenty

I Give Myself

A NEW Walter walked about the streets of Canning Town. In his corps duties he was as thorough as he had been at the coffee stall, the grocer's shop, with the tea merchant and at the sugar refinery. Now he worked under Brother Macfarlane, foreman of a shipbuilding yard, and Macfarlane watched him proudly. Walter had never lacked energy. His mother had said the trouble was to find enough for him to do. In the Army he had limitless scope. With his red jersey showing under his immaculate uniform coat, he walked along the Marsh on market days talking to people in a new way and with a new purpose, for now he had something real and lasting to offer them.

Those to whom he talked often came to hear his testimony in the open-air meeting. They listened intently. Men from the shipyards came, too. They knew that Walter Henry and Brother Macfarlane possessed strength to resist evil. They wished for this strength which they realised was not earthly. The two Salvationists never drank, never gambled, never smoked, never went out with the painted girls who, beyond the ship's pay office, waited for men to take them into a nearby pub. When the men came out they were generally miserable and penniless.

'They don't even smoke,' said Arthur Jones. Can't get Wally near a music hall. Yet he's always laughing.'

'Yes, he don't act like a crank. But to give up smokes is going a bit too far.'

'Jolly sensible if you ask me. I'll bet old Wally and his mates at the Army have fat bank accounts.'

But Walter didn't have a fat bank account. What had once been spent on cigarettes and the music hall was now set aside in the compartments of a box, one of which was labelled 'The Lord's money', a tenth of his weekly pay. Anonymously Walter prevented many widows from being hungry. Sometimes little children wore new dresses and hats. No one except Walter knew who had paid for them.

Every Saturday night with a bundle of copies of *The War Cry* and *Young Soldier* he set out for the pubs. Men from the shipyard bought papers because they believed that anything Wally sold must be good. Once a giant of a man, with muscles like a prizefighter's, who had drunk too many mugs of beer to know that Walter was only five feet four inches in height, imagined him to be an opposing giant, and ripping off his coat glowered at the Salvationist and shouted, 'I ain't afraid of you however big you are, you great elephant.'

'Good!' said Walter knowing that one punch from the real giant would knock him out.

But the whole house was against the pugilist and on the side of Walter. A tall, aristocratic man sitting quietly at a table began to chant softly: 'Two to one the little fellow. Two to one the little fellow.' Soon the men at tables and counters and even in the billiard room took up the challenge, and there was an uproarious chanting of: 'Two to one the little fellow. We guarantee two to one the little fellow.'

The big man felt rather dizzy; he turned round and stared, blinking foolishly at the chanters. 'S'all right, s'all right,' he said. 'I'll buy the lot.'

He pulled out a purse containing many golden sovereigns and offered them to Walter in exchange for all his papers, but Walter said a firm 'No!' He was not there to make money but to bring the good news of salvation to his customers. Because the men respected his principle he sold out that night, and before he left the bar-room he saw foamy glasses neglected while men sat reading around the tables.

Walter liked enthusiasm in others and he was never more moved than he was one Sunday when Elijah Cadman came to Canning Town and, dropping to his knees in the centre of the open-air ring, prayed earnestly for the people standing around. Walter knew he could not pray like Elijah Cadman, but the longing he felt to win men for God nearly choked him.

At the shipyard, fewer orders were coming in since a terrible day when a new ship, the *Albion*, had been launched. As she slid into the water she had swayed, floundered and had, as she sank, sucked men down into the waters and many of them were drowned. Newspapers carried headlines; and there was an inquiry into the reason for the accident. Walter was shocked by the fact of death. His usually ready tongue was silenced, and he was thoughtful. Had he been doing enough to lead men to God? How could anyone do enough. He must press further into the heart of the great Army whose sole purpose was the salvation of men.

Walter applied for, and was given, a book in The Salvation Army Assurance Society.

'Do you speak to all your policyholders about being saved?' inquired a sister at the corps.

'No,' said Walter honestly. 'They know I'm there to persuade them to take out a policy with the Army. But I try to do my work with them in such a way that they shall know what business is like when it is conducted by Christians.' Walter did well. He was offered a larger district, but he was being drawn closer and closer into The Salvation Army, and on Self-Denial Sunday he sat in the hall gazing at his altar service envelope and wishing his salary were larger and that he had more to give.

He put all the money he had in the envelope. Then he sat thinking. A little money, used by God, could do lot of work, but what about a life – a life in God's hands. Walter had left one job after another in order to earn more money. He had wanted to be rich. Now he saw that only God could give him the wealth he really wanted – the ability to lead others to Jesus.

He did not know about Mary collecting all day in Sydney for a farthing; and she could not see Walter drawing a pencil from his pocket and writing in a careful, open hand: 'I give myself.'

No altar service envelope had ever carried a bigger offering.

Twenty-one

Patriot of the Kingdom

WHEN Walter wrote 'I give myself' on his altar service envelope, he meant it. For Walter Henry, with all his interest in men and women, his gift for making money and his energy, enthusiasm and thoroughness were not for the world and its rewards. They were God's. 'A sacrifice,' said Walter, 'is something which a chap can use for himself, but which he offers to God who can make much better use of it.'

The Canning Town soldiers were proud of Walter; so were his father and mother. Though he would be a poor man now, instead of the rich one he had hoped to be, he would have the resources of God's Kingdom at his disposal. Walter sang earnestly and truthfully:

> *Vain, delusive world, adieu,*
> *With thy store of worthless good;*
> *Only Jesus I pursue,*
> *Who has bought me with his blood.*
> *All thy pleasures I forgo,*
> *Count but dross thy wealth and pride;*
> *Only Jesus will I know,*
> *Only Jesus crucified.*

At the training college in Clapton, East London, Walter was one of a crowd; yet there no one was just like him. He never felt lonely, for to make friends was as natural to him as to breathe. He never felt envious of the talented young men among the crowd. Some could preach eloquently; he could only say in halting language what God had done for him. Some passed their tests with ease; Walter had to work hard to get through. Some men were singers or musicians; Walter was never troubled. He had given himself and his capabilities to God and he had faith that God could use what he had offered. He could scrub the long corridors till the old boards were white; he could sell more copies of *The War Cry* than anyone. He was top on the Self-Denial collectors list. Best of all, his experience at the coffee stall gave him an understanding of men. He knew their joys and sorrows, their weaknesses and their strength. He talked easily with them in the pubs, in the shops, around the open-air stand, everywhere. He could not bear to be apart from men.

Walter considered nothing too big or too hard to tackle; nothing too small.

'Henry,' called Captain Howard, one morning, 'I want you to look over my cycle.'

'Certainly, sir!' Walter said in business-like voice. 'It's the one standing against the wall, isn't it?'

'Puncture, I'm afraid,' said the youthful captain.

Walter hurried away. Peeling off his coat and folding it on the ground beside him, he rolled up the sleeves of his jersey and set to work on the puncture. An hour later Howard found him putting the last touches to the job. He had done much more than mend one or two small punctures. The machine, thoroughly cleaned, was like a new cycle.

'Brakes needed adjusting, sir,' said Walter, 'so the work lasted a little longer.'

'Henry,' said Captain Howard, 'do you know why I asked you to mend the puncture?

'Why,' said Walter, smiling, 'because a puncture makes a bike useless.'

'No,' said Howard. 'I wanted to find out what sort of a chap you really are. This job has told me a lot more than you'll ever guess.'

He walked away, leaving Walter staring, open-mouthed, after him. 'After all a fellow can't do only half a job,' he said to himself proudly, flicking dust off the steel handle-bars.

***

The session was drawing to a close and the training college officers, weary with the innumerable arrangements connected with sending out several hundred exuberant, young men and women to all parts of the world, went about with a look of calm that belongs to hidden tension.

The cadets wondered how they could bear to wait for the commissioning, now only a few days ahead. In off-duty moments they sang cheerfully:

We're bound, we're bound,
We're bound for Timbuktu.
A sword we'll wield
In the Social or the Field,
And go to Timbuktu-oo,
And go to Timbuktu.

Sometimes the third and fourth lines were different, and the lusty voices sang:

Sunshine or shade,
We'll wear the yellow braid.

for in those days yellow was the colour of lieutenants' trimmings.

Before Commissioning Day, however, Walter and three other new cadets were summoned to the office of Colonel John Dean. Dean was the man who could preach so forcefully that, to the wide-eyed cadets, Bible characters were beside him on the platform. He could talk about the misery of life without God in such a way that a picture of this awful state seemed to be painted on the wall behind him.

The men loved him; yet in a way they stood in awe of one whom they knew as a teacher. 'He knows everything about the Bible,' they said to each other. 'If you ask a question it brings out an avalanche of knowledge.' Dean was never stumped by their questions.

Anything might happen at commissioning time, Walter thought. To one of his fellow-cadets he said: 'Wonder why he wants us.'

'Yes, why?' echoed the others, hastening along the corridor like the soldiers they were.

Walter knocked at the door. He was the first to step in, erect and immaculate, giving a swift salute. The other three, following silently, stood with throbbing hearts until Dean bid them be seated.

From behind his desk the colonel searched each face. His eyes rested on Walter when he spoke. 'You're going to Africa,' he said, 'South Africa.'

'Yes sir,' said Walter, saluting.

In those days many people knew little about South Africa. Never having visited the Cape, and hearing mainly about the missionary work where officers travelled by ox-cart, crossing mountains and rivers and living among the Zulus many miles from towns or even other Europeans, they pictured forests where lions and tigers roamed, and where men and women slept in grass-roofed huts and lived in kraals. They never pictured beautiful cities and quaint, sedate Dutch towns and villages.

Perhaps Colonel Dean knew Africa. Perhaps in his vivid description of the kind of life that might await the four cadets he may have been merely testing their willingness to endure hardship.

The picture he painted was alarming. Dangers might beset them. Gone would be the comforts of an English home and the safety of civilisation. Walter, said Colonel Dean, must be prepared to live like the Africans and, he added, picking up a pencil and pointing it at the four, 'The time may come when you will have to lose your identity.'

This time Walter did not say, 'Yes sir.'

Then Colonel Dean said, 'Are you willing to go?'

'Yes sir,' said the four.

Outside the door the young men faced each other, white and excited. 'Did you hear what he said?' demanded Walter of his companions.

'We're to lose our identity,' they said.

'That means we're not to remain British. I can't promise that. I'll go anywhere, but I could never be anything but British and on the side of the British.'

The four went quickly and solemnly to their rooms. Walter looked at the small Army flag hanging over his bed. He stared at it, and continued to stare. It was the flag of all nations. How silly of him to worry about losing his identity in Africa. He had lost it already. True he was British, but first of all he was a Salvationist; a patriot of the Kingdom of Heaven, whose citizens might live in an American skyscraper, an African hut, an igloo, or a shack, north, south, east or west. He knelt down beside the bed and offered to God his love for England. God would know what to do with it.

A few weeks later Walter sailed for Cape Town. At the Western Divisional Headquarters in Loop Street he received his appointment to Queenstown. Like Mary and Elizabeth, he looked in vain for dangers, for huts, for lions. But the quarters were in an isolated spot quite unlike Alice Street in Canning

Town, and white ants were in the table legs. One day, at breakfast, the table leg, eaten from the inside by ants, fell off, letting all the cracked crockery fall to the floor, and Walter decided there and then that a Salvation Army quarters must be even more carefully cleaned and repaired than a coffee stall.

Though towns in South Africa are far apart and one seldom sees a fellow officer, soon nearly everyone in the Western Division knew that Captain Walter Henry kept his quarters as clean as any woman, that in it there was no unrepaired furniture and that the corps, too, had undergone a cleaning-up process, men and women were being saved, backsliders returning to God.

'A good officer,' said Walter's Divisional Commander. 'I do not want to lose him.' But he lost Walter to the training college, though he gained him afterwards in another way. You see Walter's Divisional Commander was Mary's father.

Twenty-two

A Servant or a Teacher

'LET'S have a cup of tea,' Lieut-Colonel Annie Orsborn said to Mary. 'We're only a few and I must say, however strenuous the work is in session, the emptiness of the place when the girls and boys are gone is most exhausting. Make it strong, Angus!' The two women looked at each other and smiled. Mary Angus, just past 20, and Annie Orsborn, middle-aged, had so many ideals in common that scarcely any words were needed between them.

Mary was feeling rather bereft. She had surveyed the empty cubicles. Beds without sheets, with blankets neatly folded on them were a dreary sight. The last group of cadets had gone to the station, some to travel long journeys lasting two or three days. Mary pictured them going into the quiet, sedate Dutch towns, seeking out the quarters as she had done and going nervously to their welcome meetings, wondering if they could carry out successfully all the principles that had ruled them during the training days. By now she had discovered that the South African corps had none of the glamour but all the loneliness and hardship of the mission field.

Mary, with the cadets, had taken *The War Cry* and had gone from door to door selling the papers and inviting people to the meetings. At nearly every house they had been received kindly. Often *The War Cry* had been bought, and sometimes Mary had managed to start a conversation, always with the purpose of discovering whether the one visited understood the meaning of conversion.

In one home, beside the washtub, she had talked long and earnestly about God, and how the great universe, so exact, so beautiful, revealed to us something of his nature.

'Oh yes!' the woman had said joyfully.

'But,' continued Mary, 'there is nothing in a beautiful star or in a flower or even a mountain that can tell us how God desires us to act.'

'That is true,' the woman had said staring hard at Mary.

'Yet how to treat our fellow men is to God most important.'

The woman stopped work and listened more carefully. Mary had told her that Jesus had once reminded his questioners that the greatest of all God's commandments was the one which ordered us to love God with all our being and our neighbours as ourselves.

'Jesus came to teach us how God desired us to act.'

'Oh,' the weary-looking woman had said. 'I do long to know.'

'Then,' Mary had begged, 'will you kneel here and ask God's forgiveness for the times you have treated others wrongly? Will you ask him, for Jesus' sake, to show you how to live?'

The woman willingly agreed. So new was prayer to her that Mary had to pray, letting the woman repeat the words after her.

Mary had gone away from that little house with a heart nearly bursting with joy. She felt she had led a soul to God. But, alas, on the following week the woman had moved away and though Mary searched in vain, she had not found her.

Winning souls was not easy. It meant more than persuading men and women to come to the penitent form. Winning souls meant weariness and sorrow, as well as joy. Mary remembered her aching body long ago in Sydney when she had collected all day for a farthing. Soul-winning was something like that, she thought. You had to put in a lot of effort that some people might say was wasted, or you would never find the one that was lost.

All through the session Mary had taught this to her cadets. Now they were on their way to walk the long, hard way of finding men for Christ.

Mary was going to an appointment in Johannesburg, the 'golden city'. She had not visited it before, but she knew quite a lot about the fine, busy city, with its lovely suburbs. She knew also about the terrible conditions in which the poor people lived. She had seen shacks made of old sacking and little children wandering about in torn and dirty clothing.

Other people living in luxury may not have known that the low wages of their brothers and sisters made possible their tiled bathrooms and richly furnished homes. Years before, Major Allister Smith's first two converts had left Zululand and travelled to Johannesburg to earn money to pay taxes for their father's land. This the major had told them was the Christian thing to do.

A rude shock awaited Matunjwa and his friend. Educated men seemed no better than those who could scarcely write their names. Mary knew she would feel no more than a candle in her efforts to bring light to those living in darkness. She had learned that when the sower goes out to sow the seed he must leave the results to God.

But something besides the troubled world was making Mary sad as she took out the cups and saucers and poured boiling water into the teapot. She was angry with herself for having this sad feeling and sense of loss. True, she had rarely talked with Walter Henry. So little had Mary thought about marriage that she had no fixed idea in her mind about the character of the man she should choose. She had taught Orders and Regulations to cadets; she had lifted their ideas of love to a high plane. Some who had giggled every time the word courtship was mentioned, under Mary's tuition had gone away to regard marriage as the highest form of friendship, and those who had believed that one must have a husband with a handsome face now knew that his mind and spirit were more important.

But, for herself, Mary believed that a life alone was best; a life devoted to winning men and women for God. She had not realised how much she had looked forward to watching Walter drilling the cadets in the backyard, and how she had enjoyed the tremendous energy and precision with which he did his job. She missed seeing him in the lecture hall; she missed, serious though he was, his lighthearted banter. Walter had made many difficult tasks easy, for he could always laugh.

As she mused, the door opened and a fresh face peeped into the kitchen. 'Just come to say goodbye,' Walter said. Then he paused. 'Tell me, is it true about that other chap?' he asked.

'Other chap?' said Mary laughing, though she meant not to. 'What other chap?'

'Oh, is there no one?'

'Of course there isn't.'

'Well,' said Walter, 'I just wanted to be sure.' He looked at her fine face and grey eyes staring straight into his. Walter knew she was the only girl in the world for him. 'I thought,' he added soberly, 'that if there is no one else, I'd like to correspond.'

'All right,' said Mary steadily. But her heart was beating fast, and she did not feel sad any more.

'Goodbye,' he called. 'All the best.'

'God bless you,' said Mary, and when she turned to look again, the merry face was gone.

Twenty-three

Shall We be Married?

'SOME day, if you come here to St Mary's College, we can live together,' Mary wrote to Elizabeth at school. She slipped the letter into her purse and went out into the cool evening to post it. As she walked briskly along the streets her face was thoughtful. She tried to think that if Elizabeth were with her she could forget Walter.

For several years Mary had fought against the idea of being married. She felt that a husband and a home would take her mind from God. But she could not forget Walter. She constantly heard of his attention to duty and of his way of winning men over to God's side.

Every hard corps was a challenge to him, which he met with courage. His love for people became stronger as his knowledge of God increased.

Knowing nothing of this, Elizabeth read Mary's letter joyfully, counting the months when she might be able to attend St Mary's and live with Mary. What bliss!

She did not realise that, far away in Johannesburg, beyond the Draakensburg Mountains, Mary, torn in conflict, was praying, praying to be shown what to do. Of course, God does not write on walls, or change situations like a magician, but to praying people he often reveals the way they must take. At any rate Mary rose from her knees one evening and wrote Walter a letter that made him extremely happy. Mary promised to be his wife; she said she believed that, with Walter, she could do more for God than she could do without him. In fact Mary loved Walter. She wanted nothing more than to make it easier for him to be a soul-winner. There was no selfishness in Mary's love, and God honoured it.

In Port Elizabeth, on a hot day, Elizabeth came home for lunch and found, beside her plate, a postcard. On the front was a picture of Eton College. On the back were a few words: 'Have you heard my news? Mary.'

Mother told Elizabeth the story. 'Oh, fancy getting married!' said Elizabeth in a sorrowful voice. 'We were going to live together when I go to St Mary's. I shan't go to the wedding.'

She ate her lunch with her nose buried in a book about a girl who became a teacher in a convent.

***

A year later Elizabeth, on her 15th birthday, a slim schoolgirl in a white dress, stood at the door of the Town Hall in Port Elizabeth where Mary and Walter were to be married; the Army hall was too small to hold the crowd of Salvationists who wished them well. 'Great day for you, Elizabeth!' said Young People's Sergeant-Major Cherry.

'No,' said forthright Elizabeth. 'Great day for Walter.'

She slid quietly into a seat specially reserved for her in the front row where she could watch Mary and Walter, and Sheila, a corps cadet bridesmaid, with her bright curls brushed back from her forehead. Elizabeth's heart bumped with pride. She hardly realised what was happening until Commissioner Richards stood with his hand clasped over the joined hands of Mary and Walter saying reverently: 'In the name of God and The Salvation Army, I declare you to be man and wife. Whom God hath joined together, let no man put asunder.'

After their marriage Walter and Mary were appointed to Pretoria Corps. Once when Elizabeth was spending a holiday with her elder sister she heard a voice behind the closed study door. Peeping in, she found Walter by the desk with his eyes shut, talking. No one else was there, and Elizabeth ran along the passage almost afraid. But she knew Walter had been talking to God, talking as though he could see him in the silent room.

One Sunday morning, before seven o'clock, she went to knee-drill. The hall was quiet; the clear cool air of Pretoria's high altitude streamed with the sunshine into the hall. A ray of light starting from the window spread to a black scroll on the wall, illuminating it. Elizabeth tiptoed over and read the words on it. They were set out in white lettering, promising help and spiritual guidance to any needy person in Pretoria at any hour of the night or day. The declaration was signed: 'Walter and Mary Henry, servants of all for Christ's sake.'

Elizabeth wanted to be a teacher. She did not like the Army's noisy methods; the loud beat of the drum awakened nothing in her. Books were her greatest treasures. The classroom, not the Army hall, was the happiest place in her world. But as she stared at the scroll and wondered if, after all, a servant of all might, in the Army, accomplish more than a teacher. Perhaps a servant in the Army was a teacher of truth, which after all was more than geography, mathematics, languages or even literature, but that was before she met Louis.

Twenty-four

Elizabeth Watches the Servants

'LOUIS is six foot two, and handsome. He has brown eyes and light brown curly hair, and Mother says he has a virtuous face. She loves him very much. Of course we shan't marry for a long time.'

With a puzzled frown on her face Mary read Elizabeth's letter. 'She's only 18,' she said to the potatoes she was peeling. 'And she doesn't sound very happy.'

A letter from Mother made her sure that all was not well. 'Elizabeth,' said Mother, 'seems to have lost interest in everything, and I don't know how poor, patient Louis must feel. She never wants to go out with him. I am worried.'

Mary gazed wistfully at her two sleeping boys. She was lonely, for Walter's gift for raising money had led to their appointment to Bloemfontein, where Mary spent long months without him. On his motorcycle Walter travelled across the veld to the lonely farms where he was always a welcome visitor among the Boers who believed in a Salvation Army, British or Dutch, and wanted to support the work.

'That's the Army I like,' said one woman pointing to his uniform.

Of course no one could make up to Mary for Walter's absence, but she sensed that Elizabeth needed her. In the warm, silent evening with crickets beginning to chirp, she could almost hear a voice crying out, 'I want Mary … ' Winter came and the voice still seemed to be calling. Mary telegraphed home for her youngest sister.

On 4 August 1914 Elizabeth arrived in Bloemfontein. Streamer headlines in the newspaper announced: 'England declares war on Germany'. The railway station was crowded with excited people. Some were quarrelling about whether an Afrikaner could fight by the side of those who were his conquerors. World events meant nothing to Elizabeth as she hurried along the street to be with Mary. A tiny line had settled just above her freckled nose.

In the weeks that followed she helped Mary do the washing, mind the babies and scrub the floors. She was very quiet and did not read as she had always loved to do. Often Mary watched her sitting in the sun. Dreaming or listless? Mary wondered which. But she said nothing. Every day, fat letters addressed in beautiful, sweeping handwriting arrived for Elizabeth. About once a week Elizabeth sat with them before her, chewing the end of her pen and, in the end, writing only brief notes.

One lovely morning Elizabeth noticed how sad her sister seemed. 'Have I done anything to hurt you, Mary?' she asked.

'Why no, Elizabeth. But you know,' and she sat back on her heels for she was polishing the floor, 'I do miss Walter.'

'Do you?' exclaimed Elizabeth, surprised.

'Yes. When he isn't here all life seems like food without salt. You see, in a way, I do everything for Walter – even the scrubbing of a floor.'

'And do you look forward to his letters?'

'Oh yes, and when I answer them I feel I'm talking to him. Once he had an urge to turn round and come home, and that was when I was specially needing him, for Eric was ill. You see, Elizabeth, Walter and I are one now.'

'I wish, oh how I wish, I felt like that!' suddenly burst out Elizabeth. 'Louis writes pages and pages and I can't bear any of what he says. I pray over the letters every night – pray that God will help me to write a kind letter in reply and make me love Louis.'

'Elizabeth! If you don't love Louis, why are you engaged to him?'

'He is very handsome and he said he loved me. I think I didn't like to hurt his feelings.' Elizabeth was tense. Her hands were clenching and unclenching. 'And Mary, isn't it a terrible thing to break a promise?'

Still sitting on the floor, Mary said firmly, 'Yes, it is. But to spoil the life of someone is far worse.'

Elizabeth had, so far, thought only of her own life. She had determined to face anything rather than hurt Louis or break a promise. Now Mary had turned her thoughts in a new direction. To marry Louis and not to love him would be a great sin against him. Whenever Elizabeth saw a light she acted quickly.

'I'll write to him now,' she said, 'and just say the truth.'

'Yes, just say the truth,' Mary said gently, watching her sister walk away as if a great load had fallen from her shoulders.

***

Walter was home and the house was full of laughter again, except when Hardy Blain was about. Hardy's backyard and the backyard of the Bloemfontein quarters met, and Hardy could often be heard smashing beer bottles and shouting at his wife and children. One evening his wife screamed and Walter took a flying leap over the fence, confronting Hardy as, rocking, swaying and only half-dressed, he tried to swing a chair around his head.

'Hardy,' commanded Walter, 'put that down and get dressed.'

'S'not likely,' said Hardy.

'You'll do it though!' Walter said sternly.

'I'll knock your head off first,' was the reply as the chair came to rest with a crash on the table.

Sticking out his chest and walking, as he thought, boldly up to Walter, Hardy, terror of the district and nuisance to the police, rolled up his dirty shirtsleeves and demanded a fight.

But Walter, with a hand on his arm, ordered the big man to his knees, and suddenly Hardy burst into tears and wept. Walter prayed with him until he was sober. Then he took another leap over the wall and into the kitchen to talk with Mary about Hardy Blain, for whom he had been working and praying for more than a year.

'He seemed a little nearer understanding today,' Walter told Mary. But, alas, in the afternoon Walter was bringing small Walter home from the company meeting when father and son heard a deep groan coming from behind a hedge. Young Walter's hand tightened its grip on his father's. Captain Walter peered over the hedge and there in a ditch lay Hardy Blain with an empty whisky bottle beside him.

Small Walter began to cry, and no wonder, for a drunken man scarcely resembles a human being, and the little boy was more terrified of the ungainly figure than he had ever been of anything in his life.

'Don't cry, boy!' said his father. 'I'll take you home first, and then come back for Hardy Blain. You must feel sorry for him, you know, he's sick in his body, but even more sick in his soul.'

When small Walter was safely in the kitchen eating his tea, Walter senior was heaving Hardy Blain out of the ditch behind the hedge. Walter was several inches shorter than Hardy and about half his weight, but his body had not been weakened by drinking beer and he managed to drag up the drunkard and, keeping an arm around his waist (that is, as far around as a short arm would go), pull Hardy's arm around his neck and stagger along. No journey over the veld had been as difficult as this one. So weighted was Walter by the big man that he staggered and had his uniform not proclaimed sobriety he might have been rated a fellow drunkard.

Stumbling and halting one moment, then almost running the next, the two men reached Hardy's front door. Walter did not know that Elizabeth had been watching her brother-in-law and remembering the scroll hanging in the Pretoria hall with its message: 'Servants of all for Christ's sake'.

Pushing Hardy into a chair Walter said, 'Hardy, this time next Sunday you're going to be sober, and you're going with me to the Army hall.'

''S a bargain,' Hardy hiccoughed. 'Gettoutta-mesight!'

Twenty-five

In Perils and Distresses

HARDY BLAIN was sitting at the back of the hall when Captain Walter Henry invited to the penitent form those who longed to be freed from evil-doing. 'The penitent form is not the only place where you can find God,' said Walter, 'but the time to find God is the moment you hear him speak. Does he speak to you?'

'Yes!' shouted Hardy, standing up like a soldier at attention. Then, as if on parade, he stepped into the aisle, and took a right turn with much precision that onlookers felt they were hearing the voice of an Unseen One bidding Hardy 'right about face'. Once in the aisle, he clicked his heels together, standing at attention. With his eyes fixed straight ahead he seemed to be listening. Then, again as though a voice had ordered, 'By the right, quick march!' he moved swiftly forward. The sound of his measured tread and of his resolute face at the mercy seat was like music to Walter and Mary. This time they were to see the results of many months of toiling for Hardy Blain who never looked back and who, until his death many years later, remained a faithful soldier and local officer of the corps.

Through momentous years Mary and Walter served side by side. Sometimes even their friends opposed them in what they believed to be the right way of winning men and women for God. That way, for them, meant that they scarcely ever rested; they counted nothing too precious to lose if, by parting with it, they could lead one man, woman, boy or girl to God.

Sorrow came to Mary and Walter, too, as it comes to all, and lines began to appear in Mary's face, but the trouble that caused lines was more than balanced by the love of the people, by news that Sheila was running three company meetings and with her husband spending all her strength for God, by a letter from Mother, now very frail, saying that Elizabeth had been appointed to District Six.

One awful day Mary's daughter Winifred came laughing along the street with a group of schoolgirls, when she met Eric with what she called his gloomy look.

'Stop laughing, you silly thing!' he said gruffly. 'Mum's in hospital. She's dying, and we've all got to go.'

Winifred stopped laughing. In fact, for her, the sun seemed to cease shining, though in reality the heat was so great that the pavement burned her feet through her light sandals.

At the hospital, Mary's three children stood around her bed. She was so small that her body scarcely made a mound in the bed. Her eyes were closed. In turn the children kissed her and, frightened, tiptoed out. Their world was empty and dark.

Mary knew only in a vague way that they had been beside her. She was aware of a fierce pain from which she longed to be free, and of some greater pain. Was it in her mind or her spirit? How wonderful it would be to slip away to God's house of many mansions. But would there be something, someone missing in that home? She lifted a searching hand and felt over the quilt, until her fingers touched Walter's rough, warm hand. As if it were speaking from miles away in a vast realm of darkness and space, Mary heard Walter's agonised voice, 'Don't leave me, Mary!'

'Where are you?' she tried to say and couldn't. But her eyelids slowly lifted and she looked at her husband kneeling beside the bed, his head near to hers.

'No,' she whispered, 'I'll never leave you.' Then she fell into a quiet sleep from which she awakened to find the tall doctor saying in a brisk voice, 'Mrs Henry, you're a miracle.'

As soon as she was strong enough Mary was at work again, travelling long distances in the car with Walter, now a Divisional Commander. One day, they set off on a long trip through the eastern part of South Africa. They hoped, if the old car played no tricks, that they would reach Oudtshorn in time for the holiness meeting. The sun beat upon the road and clouds of dust mingled with tiny stones that pattered constantly against the car's mudguards and leaped at the windscreen. Suddenly there was a report like a gunshot and the car skidded along for several yards, crashed down the bank and lay tipsily on its side. Mary, sitting in the back, never knew what had happened. But when she regained consciousness, her first thought was: 'Walter will feel bad about this happening when he was driving.' He had clambered out of the side door, and was peering at her through a shattered window which was now over her like a roof.

'Are you all right, Mary?' he said anxiously.

'Quite,' said Mary.

When she tried to push downwards she found no power in her arms. But, with an effort, she could pull, so she wriggled herself upwards until she was in a position where Walter could lift her out.

They were still 250 miles from their destination. The brown kopjes on the undulating veld presented a lonely appearance, and Oudtshorn seemed a long way off.

'I'll find a place for you to sit down,' said Walter. 'Then I'll walk to a farm.' They looked at each other silently, both thinking of the narrow escape from death they had shared. Both thinking, 'What if I had been left alone?' Mary tried to lift her arms as Walter put his around her. They stood on the lonely veld, two strangely dishevelled people, weary, hot and shaken, with only one urge – to thank God that they were still together.

Sitting on a tree trunk, Mary waited with strained muscles and bleeding body. At last she heard a distant '*Hamba yek!*' that would be a farmer bringing his ox-wagon to take them and the broken car to the farm. She was right.

In a few more hours the car had been sufficiently repaired to be driven with care, Washed, bandaged and cheerful, Mary climbed in. Once more the battered machine chugged along the road, arriving in Oudtshorn in time to conduct the night meeting.

'I wouldn't have missed it for anything,' said Mary, when, next day, as he examined the torn ligaments of her chest, the doctor reproved her and urged a long rest.

But in three days Mary and Walter started off on another long journey.

Twenty-six

Thank You for Mary

'TACK, tack, tack, tack!' Like minute white horses galloping, Mary's fingers moved on the keys of a battered typewriter The tr-r-ring of the telephone bell was halted almost instantly by Walter lifting the receiver and saying a cheerful 'Hallo! Salvation Army here.'

Mary stopped typing so that Walter would not be disturbed. She could hear a loud, excited voice speaking at the other end of the line. 'Would The Salvation Army help me save a gifted gentleman from ruin?'

'We would – gifted or otherwise.'

'Well, this man is an aristocrat, graduate of Cambridge, and has many distinctions, but he cannot leave drink alone. He's absolutely down and out, and I believe he's staying in Burley Court.'

'That's bad,' said Walter, for he knew that Burley Court was a notorious place where respectable people did not go. 'I'll be there in 15 minutes,' he promised.

'Thank you,' said the voice.

Walter drove almost recklessly through the dark streets, reaching at last the long, tree-lined road leading to Burley Court. He saw a man dodging among the leafy shadows, like a thin wraith. 'That's the one,' Walter said aloud, and he could never have explained why he knew that the lean, dark person dodging the light was Ted Raikes. Though he hurried along the road as fast as he could, before he reached the door of Burley Court the ghostly figure had disappeared.

Walter's loud knock at the front door brought a tardy response from a woman who told him where to find Ted Raikes.

A dreary sight met Walter's eyes when, after receiving no answer to his knock, he opened the door and went in. Unkempt and white-faced, with dark hair lying damp on his high forehead, the young man sat miserably on the side of the bed.

'I've come to take you out of this place,' Walter said.

'I can't get out,' came the reply. 'I owe them money.'

'I'll settle that,' Walter said. 'You're going to one of our farms to stay till you're on your feet again.'

'But my things … .' He waved a hand toward a handsome trunk that looked like a rare piece of period furniture in a junk shop.

'I'll see that you have all that belongs to you by tomorrow night. Stay here till I've seen the landlord.'

The landlord wanted to know why The Salvation Army was interested in Ted Raikes. He was startled when Walter said, 'We want him for God; you want him for the devil.'

'Well you can't have him for God or anyone till he's paid his debts.'

'What are they?' quietly asked Walter, and laughed when a large sum was named.

'I'll give you half that,' he said taking out his pocket-book, 'and that'll be more than a lifetime in one of your rooms is worth.'

Staggered that Walter wanted Raikes enough to pay his debts, the landlord took the notes. This Salvationist was no fool, he could see, and as the landlord had much to hide from the law he thought it wiser to see as little of Walter as he could.

'I'll be back tomorrow for his trunks. Good day! I'd start an honest business if I were you.'

In the car with Walter, Ted Raikes sat in silence. Then suddenly he said, 'Why are you doing this for me?'

'Because I care what happens to men,' Walter answered.

'You care!' said Ted, more as a statement of fact than a question. He began to tell Walter of his gracious, godly parents, of his youth in England and his success at Cambridge. Then how, to obtain an honourable and responsible position, he had come to South Africa. He did not know how or why he had loosed his hold on the standard of conduct that had been his in youth. Perhaps loneliness had been a cause. At any rate he had started to drink, and drink had mastered him and, of course, he had lost his post.

'Only God can help men to go straight,' said Walter, 'and I expect you left him out of all your reckonings. But you still have time. You're young.'

As the car slowed down, a giant appeared from the wide gates of the Salvation Army farm. His healthy, tanned face and broad smile matched his shout of 'Welcome!'

'This is Captain King,' said Walter. 'He'll look after you.'

He watched the big man go off with his charge, and he was not surprised that on the following Sunday Ted Raikes came to the penitent form. For a month, until his post was restored to him, he worked on the farm. Never again did Ted forget to reckon on God.

Mary rejoiced with Walter. Once again, by serving a fellow-man they had served God.

***

Walter and Mary became known throughout South Africa. The Salvation Army officer who learned thoroughness at a coffee stall in Victoria Dock Road was welcome in the homes of rich and poor alike. Businessmen and statesmen were his friends. When King George VI visited South Africa, Mary and Walter stood with the crowd who watched him pass. Seeing the Salvation Army uniform, the

King halted to shake hands with Walter. 'I saw your General before I left England,' he said. 'I think highly of your Army.'

Walter saluted. 'It's a grand Army, your Majesty,' he said with a catch in his usually steady voice. He was too humble to realise that men and woman like himself and Mary *were* the Army, and that through the pure service of saints who work for love and not for recognition the great movement lives on.

Because they were so full, the days passed quickly, and to Mary and Walter on the eve of retirement it seemed that only yesterday they had started out together as servants of all for Christ's sake. Now their last day at Cape Town Divisional Headquarters had arrived. Mary, who had kept the books for her husband, had written down the last figure and made the last note that would make matters easy for her successor. Now she must go to their little home under the shadow of Table Mountain to prepare for a new kind of life, an easier life, perhaps, she thought, not seeing the future. Bidding Walter goodbye for the present she left him setting everything in order for the new divisional commander. He locked the desk and the cupboards. Then, with a rather wistful expression on his happy face, he gazed out over the hazy mountains toward which he and Mary so often had lifted their eyes from amid the squalor of back streets where Army open-air meetings were held.

A soft breeze ruffled his fair hair as Walter quietly knelt beside his desk and began to talk aloud as

Elizabeth had heard him talk to God in days gone by.

'Thank you, God,' were his simple words, 'for finding me and leading me all the way. And, God, thank you for Mary.'

The breeze fanned his face as he locked the office door and went into the street. Mary would be waiting for him at home.

'Thank you, God, for Mary,' he said again, quickening his pace.